PREVENTING CLASSROOM DISRUPTION

PREVENTING CLASSROOM DISRUPTION

POLICY, PRACTICE AND EVALUATION IN URBAN SCHOOLS

DAVID COULBY AND TIM HARPER

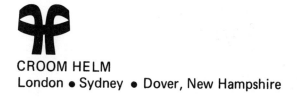

CROOM HELM

London • Sydney • Dover, New Hampshire

©1985 David Coulby and Tim Harper
Croom Helm Ltd, Provident House, Burrell Row,
Beckenham, Kent BR3 1AT
Croom Helm Australia Pty Ltd, Suite 4, 6th Floor,
64-76 Kippax Street, Surry Hills, NSW 2010, Australia

British Library Cataloguing in Publication Data

Coulby, David
  Preventing classroom disruption : policy,
  practice and evaluation in urban schools.
  1. Classroom management
  I. Title II. Harper, Tim
  371.1'024   LB3013

  ISBN 0-7099-3424-6
  ISBN 0-7099-3425-4 Pbk

Croom Helm, 51 Washington Street, Dover,
New Hampshire 03820, USA

Library of Congress Cataloging in Publication Data

Coulby, David.
  Preventing classroom disruption.

  Bibliography:p.
  Includes index.
  1. Problem children – Education – Great Britain.
2. Problem children – Great Britain – Evaluation.
3. Urban schools – Great Britain – Case studies.
I. Harper, Tim. II. Title.
LC4803.G7C68   1985   371.93   85-11359
ISBN 0-7099-3424-6
ISBN 0-7099-3425-4 (pbk.)

Printed and bound in Great Britain
by Billing & Sons Limited, Worcester.

CONTENTS

Contents

Contents

PREFACE

The Authors.

David Coulby taught for nine years mostly in East London. He established and took charge of the ILEA Division 5 Schools Support Unit for its first two years. Following this he lectured in urban education at the University of London Institute of Education. He is now head of the department of teaching studies at North London Polytechnic.

Tim Harper trained as an educational psychologist at University College, London. He worked in the London Borough of Haringey for five years and has been attached to the Division 5 Schools Support Unit in the ILEA as its psychologist for the last six years since its inception.

Although both authors are working, or have worked, for the ILEA, the views expressed in this book are entirely their own and do not necessarily represent the authority's ideas or policies.

INTRODUCTION

This book attempts to show that children who are perceived to be disruptive in their primary or secondary schools need not be excluded into a form of special provision. Neither special schools, nor the variously named disruptive units, have shown that they can make a significant improvement to the behaviour of such children once they are returned to mainstream school. However, we suggest that outbreaks of classroom disruption in primary and secondary schools can be reduced without excluding particular children. This assertion is based largely on our work in, and evaluation of, an urban support team. The team is called the ILEA Division 5 Schools Support Unit, and its method of working is described in Chapter 2. Both authors played a significant part in the development of this team. They also set up a long-term evaluation of its work. This evaluation is reported in Chapter 3.

Chapters 4 and 5 concentrate on the ways in which classrooms and schools can change to prevent incidents of disruption. Chapter 6 looks at how support teams can facilitate the integration of children perceived to have special needs. The book aims to deal in some detail with practical methods whereby exclusion to segregated provision can be avoided. To this end we present, in the course of the chapters, sections of illustrative material. These illustrations may be of work in specific contexts and with particular children; they may present case material within formats used by the unit or they may concentrate on the difficulties encountered by a team member in a certain situation. The content of this material is by no means a statistically representative sample of the Support Unit's work, but it will vividly exemplify what we mean by disruptive behaviour. To preserve the confidentiality of the participants, this illustrative material has been partly fictionalised.

Chapters 1 and 7 attempt to frame the descriptive, evaluative and practical components of the book within the wider educational debate. The way in which some children are categorised as disruptive in schools is examined. The growth of segregated provision is seen alongside the apparently opposite trends towards comprehensivisation and the integration of pupils perceived to have special needs.

We would like to acknowledge the help of past and present members of the Schools Support Unit with whom we discussed the ideas and practices presented in this book. In particular we would like to thank those who allowed aspects of their work to be presented as illustrative material. We would also wish to acknowledge the help of the schools and educational services of ILEA Division 5 who cooperated in the establishment of the team, and all those teachers who patiently filled in the apparently endless sequence of questionnaires which were essential to our evaluation. We owe special thanks to David Lane and his colleagues at the Islington Educational Guidance Centre for discussions with them. Dr. Peter Mortimore of ILEA Research and Statistics encouraged and guided our evaluation; our thanks are due to him and to his staff for help with running our data through the computer. Our typist, Mrs. Sibylle Muirden, transformed our manuscript into a neat typescript with speed and precision. Additional thanks to her.

Finally, in recognition of the importance of the work of the past, present and future members of the support team, we would like to dedicate this book to the memory of Nigel Pryor.

Chapter 1

THE CONCEPT OF CLASSROOM DISRUPTION

1.1 Ploughman's Lunch.

In the 1970's the education system in England and
Wales created a new category of pupil, "the disruptive child". It was rather like the creation of the
ploughman's lunch made famous in the film of that
name. What now seems like a traditional and appeti-
zingly earthy part of our gastronomic culture,
stretching back into the mists of medieval folklore,
was actually a concept put together by an advertising
agency less than fifteen years ago. Similarly, the
word disruptive is now applied by educators to pupils
as if it signified a well-known type of child. The
category now has the authority of the familiar, of
the educationally accepted. It is this acceptance
that we wish to challenge. At the outset it might be
best to assert boldly that there is no such thing as
a disruptive pupil. Certain pupils behave disruptively in some lessons, with some teachers, in some en-
vironments at certain times of the day or week. Some
pupils behave disruptively in corridors, playgrounds
and staircases. Do any pupils behave disruptively
with all teachers? in all lessons? in all contexts?
And if they did, would disruptive any longer be the
best way of describing them? Disruptive is a word
better applied to forms of behaviour or to situations
than to pupils. Most labels simplify life for the
person doing the categorising. For the person who is
categorised, however, they may have pernicious and
long-term consequences.
      There is more here than semantics. If we per-
ceive a situation to be disruptive, then this is a
temporary state of affairs, and one which involves
several participants. If we perceive behaviour to be
disruptive, then this is something which can change
into other more appropriate behaviours. But if we
perceive a pupil to be disruptive, this is somehow
something to do with his/her personality or nature.

3

This means that we are more likely to regard it as
permanent and difficult to change. We will probably
then see any incident in which a "disruptive pupil"
is involved as caused by him/her rather than as a
clash between various participants within a specific
context. In other words, now that the category of
disruptive exists, it is easy for particular pupils
to be stigmatised, but it is actually more difficult
to conceptualise ways of developing change in behaviour, or of diminishing the frequency of disruptive
incidents. Why should anyone waste time trying to
develop plans for change and improvement when it is
clear that it is the child who is disruptive? The
existence of the category "disruptive pupil" both in
the provision of a local education authority and in
the mental set of educators, may then actually serve
to inhibit methods of cutting down disruption in
mainstream primary and secondary schools.
It is possible to ask how "the disruptive pupil" was created. This question may be answered in
two ways: by reference to the way in which the category of disruptive pupils came into existence in the
education system of England and Wales; or by reference to the way in which specific children acquire
the label whilst in mainstream primary and secondary
schools. These two aspects of the question will each
be considered in some detail.

1.2 The Creation of the Category.

Children have always indulged in disruptive behaviour in schools. We say this blandly in order not
to give the impression that there is no such thing
as disruptive behaviour, or that particular children do not have a predilection for it. Nor do we
wish to assert that bullying, racism, rudeness,
theft and vandalism are really quite acceptable.
They are no more acceptable in a school than in any
other institution. Indeed, many writers, following
Durkheim, have seen the socialisation of children
into generally accepted patterns of behaviour to be
one of the main tasks of the school. Particularly in
infant schools, the encouragement of co-operation,
good working habits, friendliness and mutual tolerance and respect are significant aspects of the
work of the teacher. This is sometimes regarded as a
rather sinister form of social control. It is necessary at this stage, then, to make a working distinction between socialisation and social control.

The concept of classroom disruption

Socialisation of young children takes place in the family and the school. It serves to allow young people to accommodate to society. This need not mean that they accept unquestioningly all its values, practices and institutions. Rather, they should learn to work co-operatively, tolerantly and with determination to change and develop those elements which they consider to be incommensurate with human needs. Preventing bullying and exploitation in schools, for instance, and persuading children that this is an unpleasant type of activity may be seen as a valid form of socialisation. However, what may be excused as socialisation in many schools, is perhaps more correctly seen as systematic social control. Unquestioning obedience, uniformity of appearance, regimentation, and unflinching patience are examples of social control exerted over pupils in many schools. We discuss some of the consequences of, and alternatives to, rigid social control in this and succeeding chapters.

Disruptive behaviour has been perceived and treated differently by teachers at different stages of educational history. In the late nineteenth century, after the introduction of universal compulsory schooling, it was likely to be seen as morally reprehensible, bad, even evil. Corporal punishment was a method frequently employed to attempt to control such behaviour and punish the sinners. In the twentieth century, medical and psychodynamic explanations became more socially acceptable, indeed, fashionable. Children behaved inappropriately because there was something wrong with them; either they were "mentally defective", or they were sick in some way. Maladjustment, as a category, developed out of this paradigm. Children who did not conform were perceived as maladjusted, because their home life was stressful, they had not received sufficient maternal affection at an early age, they were acting out oedipal anxieties, or whatever. Treatment was to separate them from their less deviant peers, and to educate them together in an ethos of "stern love". This philosophy can still be found in some schools for maladjusted pupils in England and Wales today. However, there has been a trend to refer to these schools fewer children remarkable for their interesting middle-class problems, and many more of those whose violent, unruly behaviour is more popularly associated with working class and black groups (Bowman, I., 1981). This has meant that the philosophy of these schools has been increasingly difficult to put into practice.

As the category of maladjusted was increasingly
stretched to allow the incorporation of boisterous
working-class youth within the segregated educational provision, a new growth area was being established. These same children were also being referred to ESN (M) schools in large numbers. These
referrals were more likely to be on the basis of
perceived behaviour than of their academic performance (Tomlinson, S., 1981). Between 1950 and 1977,
according to the DES, the number of children in ESN
(M) schools in England and Wales rose from 15,173 to
55,698. Over the same period the number in schools
for the maladjusted exploded from 467 to 10,452.
        Towards the end of this period a new explana-
tion of disruptive behaviour, based on social learning theory, began to emerge. Children were seen as
having learnt patterns of behaviour according to the
contingent reinforcements of their specific social
contexts. Some of the segregated special schools began to develop methods of education and treatment
based on these theories. This involved positive reinforcement and rewards for appropriate behaviour,
sometimes organised around token economies. At the
same time the term disruptive came to be used, sometimes alongside and sometimes in place of previous
labels such as maladjusted or disturbed. Despite the
rapidly rising numbers of places available in special schools, there was pressure to segregate even
more children, and to exclude them quickly without
the lengthy embarrassment of special education procedures. Tutorial centres, guidance units, support
units, sanctuaries, alternative classes, opportunity
groups, and a host of other euphemistically named
provisions sprang up both on and off the sites of
mainstream schools. What had happened to the schools
of England and Wales since the 1944 Education Act
that had necessitated the exclusion of so many
children first into special school provision and
then, additionally, into the various units?
        One noticeable change which had taken place in
many local education authorities was the progress
towards comprehensive schooling. There is no obvious
reason why this move towards greater educational
equality should lead to disruptive behaviour in
classrooms. Yet Hargreaves has pointed to some of
the difficulties that beset the implementation of
the policy which, significantly, was seen as providing "grammar schools for all" (Hargreaves, D.,1982).
The skills and flexibilities of secondary modern
schools and their teachers tended to be undervalued
and neglected in the new (often amalgamated) compre-

hensive schools. In the attempt to stamp the grammar
school ethos and the grammar school curriculum on
all children, it is possible that the potentialities
for friction and boredom were increased. This is not
to imply that children from secondary modern schools
were less "intelligent" than those from grammar
schools, or less capable of performing well at a ri-
gorous curriculum. Rather, there was a mismatch between the needs and interests of the children and the
expectations of those teachers who came to control
the new institutions. Institutions which practise
streaming and which value elitist knowledge and examination success may alienate those pupils whom
they label as less successful.

In some authorities comprehensivisation was
followed by the introduction of restrictions on the
use of corporal punishment. Some teachers and heads
assumed that this would leave them with no coercive
threat with which to enforce discipline. As the ILEA,
for instance, moved towards completely banning corporal punishment, there was pressure from many people, especially in secondary schools, for some alternative to be provided. The planning and implementation of ILEA's vast disruptive units programme may
well have been a response to this (Reece, M., 1983).
The unpalatable fact seems to be that some teachers,
when deprived of the right to beat their pupils, determined that the only way to deal with them was to
exclude them from the mainstream school. Local education authorities seem to have been surprisingly
willing to collaborate in this process.

It is perhaps appropriate to mention briefly
the wide context within which the category of disruption was created. In the early seventies popular
discourse, orchestrated by the media, adopted the
language of crisis. Two notable crises were "the
urban crisis" and "the youth crisis". The urban crisis was a headline formula for the run down of many
of Britain's inner cities, associated with the exo-
dus of industry, commerce, and the prosperous section of the population. The inner cities had become
areas of concentration for poverty, "social problems", and crime. Classroom disruption in inner city
schools would then be located within a specific icon-
ography of popular conceptions. The crisis of youth
concerned the moral panic about the highly visible,
and occasionally violent, activities of some youth
subcultures such as skinheads or punks. "The disruptive pupil" could easily be inserted into this
familiar media demonology. The creation of "the disruptive pupil" arose against a background of esca-

lating youth unemployment and urban decline, but
these factors were re-interpreted through a conser-
vative climate of concern, which perceived them as
issues of undisciplined young people, seaside riots,
mugging, glue-sniffing, and so on.

We are at pains to avoid giving the idea that
the amount or intensity of classroom disruption actually increased during the 1970's. It is likely that
the change came in the relative tolerance of teachers who, concerned with the academic progress of the
majority, were less able to deal flexibly with the
distracting, counterproductive activities of a minority. However, at one point in the early 1970's, the
teacher shortage in many urban areas was so severe
that schools were severely constrained in their educational activities. It may well be that during this
period there was a higher level of disruptive behaviour in some schools. This could then be reformula-
ted by some teachers, newspapers, and popular concern as yet another aspect of the crisis of city
youth. Instead of more and better teachers, a pressure developed for the short, sharp shock model of
custodial care and for segregated disruptive units.

The growth of disruptive units in England and
Wales occurred at the initiative of local education
authorities. Probably responding to similar pressures, they copied expeditious forms of provision
which were seen to have developed in other areas.
There was no central instruction or guidelines from
the Department of Education and Science. A document
from Her Majesty's Inspectorate described and cata-
logued the developments, expressing neither approval
nor disapproval (HMI, 1978). Their dubious legality
under the 1944 Act remained unquestioned until the
Rampton Report (DES, 1981, p.50). It is surprising
that their legality has rarely been challenged in
that they provide a method of excluding children
from their mainstream classrooms, sometimes for several years, without the safeguards of a special
education referral. A child can be placed full-time
in a unit often simply at the request of the headteacher with or without the agreement of other teachers. The risks of arbitrariness, or even victimi-
sation are apparently unchecked either by the
scrutiny of outside professionals, the possibility
of DES intervention, or by rights provided to parents and children in law.

This was the background against which the units
developed, and the category of "disruptive pupils"
became institutionalised. According to the DES the
number of units rose from 23 in 1970 to 239 in 1977.

The concept of classroom disruption

A survey by ACE*in 1980 indicated that there were 439 units in the two thirds of LEA's who responded to their enquiries. In ILEA alone, there were 226 units, catering for 3,800 pupils (Booth, T., 1982, p. 28). What is surprising is that the authorities were able to proliferate these institutions during a period of severe financial stringency. Nevertheless, by the beginning of the 1980's the pattern of separate provision had been established, and the category of "disruptive pupil" had come into institutional existence. Given that the units (and the special schools also) were being provided, it was unlikely that the teachers in mainstream schools would be so churlish as to fail to find children to exclude into them. The existence of "disruptive pupils" had become an accepted part of school life.

*Advisory Centre for Education

1.3 How Schools Can Create Disruptive Pupils.

In Chapters 4 and 5 we will be looking at the more positive aspect of this question, namely how schools can minimise the amount of classroom disruption. However, since it is our insistence that disruptive behaviour is generated by schools rather than being inflicted on them, it is necessary to examine the processes whereby this comes about. These processes may be studied under four main headings: curriculum, pedagogy, organisation, and peer group. There is obviously some overlap between these headings.

1.3.1 Curriculum. If the knowledge and curriculum of the school are seen to be the exclusive product and prerogative of an elite, then many working-class and black children are likely to perceive them as separate from, and potentially alien to, their own experience. If the culture of the child is belittled or ignored in school, whilst a white, middle-class alternative is revered and made the criteria of academic and economic success, then resentment against the epistemology of the teachers may be far from irrational. Working class children, black pupils and girls may all find themselves subjected to an inferior, or even hostile, curriculum.

For example, the curricula of schools in England and Wales still contain many important elements of overt and covert racism. An example of the former is the reading scheme Pirates, where the villains are the black pirates. This scheme is a favourite for use with "remedial" children, who stand a chance of being black themselves, or of being "disruptive", or

9

both. If a child is expected to learn to read through books which reinforce negative stereotypes about his/her colour, then she/he may perceive the whole process of education as an attempt to demean and degrade. Covert racism is evident in the way in which literature and science are seen as exclusively the product of one continent. The achievements of black people in the world, as well as in the UK, are still too little stressed in urban multi-cultural schools.

Gender stereotypes are also encouraged at an early age by reading material such as the Ladybird scheme. At secondary school it is still too often the norm that boys do craft, design and technology, and computer studies, whilst girls do domestic science and office practice. However, girls also learn from an early age in both the school and the family that an important component of femininity is passivity. Girls then cannot express any resentment generated by the sexist curriculum without undermining their notions of their own sexuality. That these controlling notions are themselves partly the product of the sexist curriculum constitutes something of a double-bind. The curriculum is part of the controlling ideology of patriarchy, which tends to preclude on the part of girls the direct expression of anger and resentment. Disruptive behaviour is more common among boys than among girls by a factor of three (see Chapter 3).

Forms of disruptive behaviour may seem remote from the nature of the school curriculum: bullying younger children does not seem like a considered response to being subjected to middle-class knowledge. There does not seem to be a direct connection between disruptive activity and epistemological revolt. Nevertheless, the often boring, irrelevant and patronising nature of the school curriculum plays its part in the process of disillusionment with school. To ignore this disillusionment and always to seek the cause of disruptive behaviour in the psychopathology of individual pupils is to inhibit the necessary improvement in the curriculum currently offered to all children.

1.3.2 Pedagogy. The way in which teachers present lessons can facilitate or discourage classroom disruption. In Chapter 4 we consider this matter in some detail, so let us merely introduce the subject here by an extreme and doubtless atypical example. The extreme case again allows the percepttion to be made that classroom disruption is not an irrational form of activity indulged in by "dist-

urbed" pupils, but an active and meaningful response
to the classroom context and its interpersonal relations. Take the teacher who arrives late for a lesson, hands back a pile of unmarked books, and embarks
on a lesson which, to the pupils, seems to lack both
preparation and interest. The pupils may well lose
confidence in the teacher, but further their commitment to the enterprise of schooling will be that bit
weakened. At first this may lead only to behaviours
which are incompatible with the aims of the teacher,
such as private conversations, horseplay, or comic
reading. But cynical and anti-authority behaviours
and attitudes will also be developed, which may subsequently spread to other lessons, or to the corridors and playground. The example here may be extreme,
but a similar case could be made for other teacher
behaviours, such as using sarcasm, overlooking bullying, personal rudeness or physical punishment.

The intention here is not to attack teachers,
but to assert that they play a part in the generation
of disruptive incidents. Disruptive incidents cannot
be spuriously explained as the result of having "disruptive pupils" in a classroom: they occur in social
contexts, and as a consequence of preceding events
in which teachers have participated. What we are saying here may be seen to be less critical if formulated into the more authoritarian language of the
staffroom, where it is accepted that some teachers
have better class control than others.

1.3.3 <u>School Organisation.</u> Many school rules, such
as those concerned with dress, appearance and
superficial conduct such as chewing gum, seem designed to provide a multitude of opportunities for
defiance and confrontation. It might perhaps be argued that if pupils are persistently getting into
trouble for not wearing a tie, they will not risk any
more serious challenges to authority. But an endless
succession of petty disputes between teachers and
pupils over superficial issues is hardly likely to
encourage a positive climate of educational work.
(School rules are discussed in more detail in Chapter 5.)

This leads to the further organisational issue
of consistency between school staff (and here it is
necessary to include playground and ancillary helpers) with regard to endorsing and enforcing the
rules. The behaviour of some staff in terms of punctuality, smoking, dress and language may indicate
that they actually hold the rules they enforce in
contempt. Others may prefer tacitly to ignore brea-

ches in rules which they consider to be too rigid or petty. School organisations are likely to increase the incidence of disruptive behaviour not only by insisting on the implementation of unnecessary rules, but also by failing to provide opportunities for discussion and consultation between members of staff concerning the regulations they are meant to enforce.

Perhaps an even more significant school organisation element in the creation of disruptive behaviour is streaming (Corrigan, P., 1979). It is necessary to include here those banding arrangements which offer a palpably inferior curriculum to those whom teachers consider to be less able. Particularly in secondary school, there may be some pupils who perceive that their teachers consider them to have little chance of examination success, and that the rest of their time in school is to be devoted to trivial and make-work activities. They may then turn their attention to other interests which are either irrelevant to schoolwork, or directed against teachers and lessons. Schools sometimes blame this on the examination system which prevents most sixteen-year-olds from leaving school with a positive record of achievement. But schools determine which examinations should be taken, and how teaching groups should be organised.

There is often a degree of confusion between those pupils considered least able, and those perceived as troublesome in lessons. It has been shown, for instance, that behaviour is main criterion which heads use in referring children to ESN (M) schools rather than academic performance (Tomlinson, S., 1981). Learning failure, however, precedes placement in schools for the maladjusted for the majority of primary children. It is, nevertheless, impossible to suggest that there is always some inherent connection between low academic achievement and indulgence in disruptive behaviour. We would suggest that in many cases it is more likely that lack of academic success leads to boredom, frustration and the search for other means of establishing self- and peer-esteem. At the same time, there is a school organisational element which speeds up this process. Referral to remedial classes or ESN (M) schools as well as placement in the lower academic streams or bands may result from a child's being considered difficult and likely to inhibit the work of the "bright" groups, rather than from any lack of ability. (It is easy, in these processes, to confuse ability and attainment.) Much disruptive behaviour in non-academic secondary classes centres around a group of pupils whose needs, in terms of being taught basic skills, have not been met. These are then stigmatised, grouped together, and subjected to an inferior curriculum, often with poor equipment and with either the least effective teachers, or the staff disciplinarian.

Remedial and special classes , then, in both primary and secondary schools, provide further facilities for the creation of disruptive behaviour. This applies specifically to full-time, semi-permanent provision rather than to specialised help in the ordinary classroom. But where the segregation is rigid and the stigmatisation overt, disruption across the whole school is more likely to be increased than decreased by the existence of such provision. Certainly, many pupils prefer to attend these classes and some may benefit from them (though clear, long-term evidence for this is yet to be brought forward). Despite this, such classes can too easily become concentrations of disruptive behaviour. In some schools this can be pre-empted by isolating the provision: the rejection of the pupils is then symbolised by their relegation from the main building into an annexe or pre-fab. In less isolated provisions, the negative effects of the formation of such a class are likely to be mediated through the peer group. The artificial concentration of labelled and disaffected children is a ready focus for rule-breaking in the playground and on corridors; their anti-authority attitudes may be attractive to other adolescents; their examples of non-attendance, unpunctuality and defiance hold out an alternative, colourful model readily available for peers to adopt. We are not insisting here that such classes are a Bad Thing per se (though this is argued later), but rather that, on the whole, they are as likely to be an organisational method of facilitating disruption as of ameliorating it.

Other organisational aspects of a school which can influence the frequency of disruptive incidents concern lunchtime, playtime, and break supervision, and arrangements for corridors and staircases during free time and lesson changes. The old urban school with its collection of echoing staircases so difficult to supervise, is almost as much an invitation to disruptive behaviour as modern, narrow corridors and flimsy building materials. These features may facilitate disruption if too many lesson or room changes are timetabled, or if no teacher is responsible for supervision. Such potentiality for disruption concerns all teachers as, even when it occurs out of

class, it can spill over into lessons through late-
ness and the continuation of an excited atmosphere.
The practice of expelling children from school buil-
dings three hours per day into playgrounds often
dominated by a rugged game of football, and perceived by many pupils as hostile, boring, and wind-
swept, hardly encourages a positive attitude to the
school and what it has to offer, though it may provide an essential respite for hard-pressed teachers.

Contact with parents is another aspect of
school organisation which may have a bearing on
classroom disruption. Many schools are presently attempting to make their contacts with parents more
frequent, positive and reciprocal. It is worth em-
phasising that this is incommensurate with the common stance of blaming parents for their children's
disruptive behaviour. There is still a tendency in
many schools, after a particularly stormy episode,
to summon parents to the head's office, in the hope
that giving them a tongue-lashing will prove more
effective than administering the same to their off-
spring. In such parental "interviews" the values of
the school and of the home can be brought into
sharp opposition. The results can range from sullen
resentment to mutual blame. Even if parents are prepared to wave a stick for the school, this can sometimes lead to absenteeism rather than reformation on
the part of the pupil. Relationships with parents
are too often a consequence of those deficit models
of working-class and black families (discussed below) still prevalent in many staffrooms.

Finally, the response of school organisations
to support and assistance may also influence the
incidence of disruptive behaviour. Classroom disruption places teachers, particularly the young or
inexperienced, under stress. They may need tangible
assistance, advice, or simply opportunities to talk
things through. This assistance can come from experienced colleagues within a school, or from outside agencies such as Schools Psychological Service, or support teams, such as that described in
Chapter 2. However, it is, unfortunately, those
teachers, and indeed schools, most in need of help
who, from unwillingness to reveal what they may
construe to be failure, are often least likely to
ask for, or accept, support and advice. An atmosphere in which staff are afraid to discuss disruptive incidents for fear of seeming inadequate
("they never behave like that in my lessons") may
then serve to perpetuate disruptive behaviour. Similarly, a school which is defensive about the in-

volvement of outside agencies may well be disguising, even from itself, the nature and extent of its difficulties.

1.3.4 The peer-group. We have argued that the policy of considering disruptive pupils, in isolation from the context of disruptive incidents, is ill-considered. We have emphasised rather that many elements in school life contribute to the generation of classroom disruption. We have pointed to the contribution which the adults make to disruptive incidents, but of course, children, even those who are not "disruptive", are also involved. Sometimes the selection of one or two "disruptive pupils" from a class can be somewhat arbitrary. Often, when the one or two pupils who are considered to be most "disruptive" are removed from a class, the level of disruption is only momentarily diminished.

School provides for children a much wider (and often more lively) experience than that constituted by the teachers and the curriculum. Children go to school to see each other. The intricacies of pupil social life - chat, games, fights, pecking orders, teasing - provide a separate alternative curriculum for each school day. From this social life, as well as from family and wider controls, emerge concepts of self and other people. The emerging behaviour pattern of a child may be encouraged and reinforced by the praise, esteem, notice, laughter, or even negative attention of the peer group. Some of these behaviour patterns may include classroom disruption. The pupils concerned, of course, and indeed their peer group, are unlikely to conceptualise events in this way (Rosser, E., and Harre, R., 1976).

In the short term a group can manipulate a child by a dare, or by intimidation, to perform some action likely to lead to amusement, distraction or embarrassment. In the long term, manipulation may be less contrived, but peer responses and interactions, repeated and varied in different settings, are likely to encourage the development of those all too familiar classroom roles - the clown, the bully, the victim, the idiot, the one who argues cheekily with teacher, tough guy, glamour girl, the one who is really only interested in pop music/chess/computers, etc. Teachers rarely collude to the extent of taking these roles at face value. It is the reinforcement and encouragement which pupils receive from their peers for acting out such roles in disruptive situations in class which serve to assist the creation of the "disruptive pupil".

1.4 Illustrative Material: Jason, a Boy with no Friends.

Jason was referred because of "Rudeness to adults" and "Asocial behaviour in class and especially in playground", as a first year junior. His new teacher was having problems and believed that they were to do with Jason's "confused home situation". When specific behaviours were discussed, three seemed to be important: "hits children in free situations"; "hits children in playground"; "pokes children when in group activity".

Contact was made with Jason's mother to encourage contact with the school, but at the same time further investigations were continued in order to understand Jason's classroom behaviour. In interviews with the headteacher, the classteacher, and his teacher for the previous year, the picture emerged of a lively, but isolated boy. His classteacher felt that, although he was "very bright" and could read well, he had "no friends", was "out on a limb, some days fine, but other days all out of order". She repeated "he has no friends. He is less trouble when given individual tasks". His teacher from the previous year had a similar view: Jason "hardly ever related to anyone, had no friends". "Towards the end of last year there began to be complaints about Jason in the playground". She summed him up as "an unhappy child with no friends". Classroom observations confirmed Jason's isolation from his peer group, and his occasional violent behaviour to other children.

After the assessment period, the teacher and headteacher had a different view of Jason from that at referral. They saw his difficulty to be largely that of his exclusion from his peer group, but that he was actually reinforced by the attention paid to him as the "odd man out". This only served to deepen his isolation and loneliness. It was felt that this vicious circle might be broken by intervening in school to try to improve Jason's relationships with his peer group, and to help him make friends.

1.5 The Consequences of the Creation of "The Disruptive Pupil".

Whilst accepting that classroom disruption is often entirely antithetical to the positive, educative task of schools, we do not accept that responsibility or blame for such events can be placed exclusively upon individual children. From this, it follows

that we are critical of those theoretical accounts
which legitimate the blaming of individual pupils
(these are considered in Section 1.6 below), and
also of those methods of treatment or remediation
which focus exclusively on one child. As mentioned
above, these treatments have developed through punishment and therapy into institutional segregation.
These approaches may all still be discerned at present, indeed, even in the past they tended to overlap. Most segregated provisions would claim to have
some therapeutic influence. Likewise, it could be
argued that neither segregated provision, nor in
some instances therapy, are entirely without their
punitive overtones. The main present day provision
for pupils who are considered to be disruptive involves segregated provision in either special school
(maladjusted, ESN [M]), special unit (sanctuary,
etc.), or special (remedial) class. As indicated at
the beginning of the chapter, there are large numbers
of children thus classified and segregated in England and Wales. They may attend the various provisions full- or part-time, and on either a strictly
temporary or effectively permanent basis. We will
refer to all these provisions as segregation. The
major consequences of the creation of "the disruptive pupil" are connected with the further increase
in segregation, which has resulted. We will consider the effects of this on those children who are
segregated out of the mainstream schools, and on
those who remain there. The wider role of segregation in education and society can then be considered.

Much of what we argue has particular reference
to the off-site units for "disruptive pupils" which
have already been widely criticised (Whitty, G.,
1981), but we resist the facile tendency of sepa-
rating these from other elements of special provision. The fact that these units are not recognised
special schools may be administratively convenient,
but - except in the general inferiority of their
facilities - they are in no way intrinsically different from other special schools. On the one hand
this means that many of the criticisms which have
been levelled against the units could equally be
made against many special schools. On the other hand
it means that recent policies for integrating designated handicapped children into mainstream schools
(the timid 1981 Education Act and succeeding Circular 1/83) should apply equally to those in the most
recent and least official category.

1.5.1 <u>The Segregated Pupils.</u> It is interesting to ask why the disruptive units were set up outside the structure of special schools, and what advantages this arrangement has for teachers and administrators. The first obvious advantage is financial. Since these units are somehow not allowed to be schools, though they are often as large as some special schools in terms of numbers of pupils and teachers, then there is no need to pay an expensive headteacher salary. Most teachers in charge of units are happy to accept a Scale 3 or 4. Since the units are not officially special, then further savings can be made by parsimoniously denying teachers a special school allowance. The absence of a headteacher is a further advantage, in that a humble teacher-in-charge does not have the official power or the accepted status to argue with decisions made by administrators or "real" headteachers of mainstream schools.

The advantage of the flexible units over the official special school is most obvious at the stage of referral. The time-consuming special education procedures, now involving the drawing up of statements, can be completely swept aside. These procedures provide valuable safeguards for pupils and parents. It is not possible for a teacher or head simply to send a child to special school. Checks must be made on their judgements by other professionals: parents have a right to be consulted in the process, to scrutinise reports, express choices, and, if necessary, appeal against decisions. Perhaps because special school waiting lists were too long, perhaps because psychologists were perversely resistant to the advice of headteachers with regard to expeditious special school placement, these referral procedures are rarely required for placing children in disruptive units. The pretext for this is often that such placement is part-time or only a temporary measure. In practice, children can spend many years of their school careers in a unit. This means that pupils can be excluded from mainstream schools merely at the request of their schools. The possibilities for unfairness and arbitrariness have already been mentioned. Parental consultation can be reduced to a meeting to inform them that the school thinks it best for their child to attend a unit. Any objection is countered by a (sometimes) subtle threat of suspension. The parents rarely take up their option to appeal to the Education Office. The first effect of placement on a segregated pupil can be a quite valid sense of injustice.

The concept of classroom disruption

By the processes of referral, assessment and placement, whether in special school or unit, the segregated pupils are stigmatised in their own eyes, and in those of their families and peers. The stigma consists in feeling not only rejected, but that they are officially different from the rest of their age group, different to such a degree that they can no longer be allowed to keep company with them, but must rather be sent to strange institutions (often with fiercely negative local associations). Under this pressure, children may initially reject the rejection, and insist they do not care or, pitifully, they may promise to reform if only they can stay with their peers. In front of their families and friends, they may feel humiliated, their worth degraded. Later, through familiarity and through contact with similarly stigmatised peers, they may come to accept the label that has been placed on them. They may come to see themselves as stupid or mentally deranged in some way. The internalisation of the stigma may lead to a narrowing down of aspirations or a rejection of official institutions.

Commentators, including HMI and ILEA (Mortimore P. et al., 1983) are agreed that units, particularly those off the site of a mainstream school, offer their pupils an inferior curriculum. This is partly because small staffs cannot always cover the range of subjects available in a large primary or a secondary school. It is also a further consequence of setting the units up on the cheap. Premises are often of poor quality, equipment scarce, and there are rarely such facilities as science laboratories or craft rooms. But even in special schools, which are rarely the victims of parsimony, the curriculum is normally a restricted and down-graded version of that available in mainstream schools. The most severe effect of this on segregated pupils is that they do not receive as adequate an education as children in mainstream schools. We are not suggesting that they are not given concern, personal guidance, and excellent attention to their needs as human beings: only that they are not allowed to learn as much about as wide a range of subjects as mainstream pupils. At worst, they can be exposed to the remedial subjects plus table tennis curriculum, spending much of the day on repetitive, pedestrian exercises. The further effect of these curriculum restrictions is that they are only likely to take a small number of public examinations, if any. It may be argued that, even without segregation, these pupils were hardly likely to gather the glittering prizes of the education system.

This negative assumption, however, is no grounds
for their having their opportunities institutionally
restricted. A recommendation that a pupil spend the
last few years of compulsory schooling in a unit or
school for the maladjusted may be a sentence to
leave school with inferior qualifications and, as a
result, with diminished opportunities in the labour
market.

A further consequence of segregation is that
pupils are sent to classes where their peers do not
consist of the representative mixture they might
hope to meet in mainstream schools. The pupil may
well be influenced by the behaviour, attitudes and
expectancies of stigmatised peers in special schools
or units. If the aim is to help pupils perceived to
be disruptive to be more like other children, then
it is a rather strange procedure to place them in a
peer group which has been selected on the basis that
it is not like other children at all (Topping, K.J.,
1983).

1.5.2 The pupils who remain in mainstream schools.

It is assumed that pupils who are not sent to
special classes, units, or schools, can only benefit
from the exclusion of those who are. Teachers can
now get down to the business of engaging pupils
with the curriculum, without everything being
spoiled by one or two trouble makers. We have suggested that once one head is lopped off the Hydra
of disruption, others may spring up to take its
place. Nevertheless, the evidence of segregated
provision does have an influence on the education
of those never sent to it which might not, however,
be entirely for the good. At the very least mainstream pupils live their school lives under the
overt or covert threat that, if they do not conform to the requirements of teachers, there are
other, less congenial institutions to which they
can be summarily sent. The occasional disappearance
of one pupil may serve to concentrate the minds of
others.

A further effect is that mainstream pupils are
given a distorted impression of the nature of human
normality. The separation from all children perceived to have special needs is relevant here, not
only those labelled as disruptive. Children in mainstream schools hardly ever share their lessons with
blind, partially hearing, or cerebral palsied children. These handicapped children are cosmetically
removed from most primary and secondary schools.
Those who do not learn quickly, and those who be-

have differently from the accepted pattern also do
not stay long in the mainstream school. One effect
of this is for children and young people to regard
handicap or unusual behaviour as strange, slightly
threatening, and somehow beyond their own immediate
experience and, indeed, concern.(Consider the collo-
quial use of words like 'sick' or 'spastic' among
many children, or for that matter, adults.) Their notion of acceptable human appearance, performance, and
behaviour is one which has been carefully scrutinized
by the nature of their peer group, to exclude the
exceptional child. Another effect is that they do not
know how to deal with handicapped people or unusual
behaviour when they meet them in later life: they
are likely to respond with incompetence and embarrassment. The distorted version of human life too
easily accepted in society is partly the effect of
people not having been educated alongside their less
fortunate or handicapped peers.

A third effect of segregation on the non-segre-
gated pupils is that mainstream schools do not need
to adapt. There is a way in which much disruptive behaviour can be conceptualised as a response to the
circumstances of the school. To carry this analysis
a little further, we could say that.many pupils resist the petty rules, the curricular irrelevances and
the teacher tyrannies that can be experienced daily
in some schools. If some of the pupils engaging in
resistant activity can be summarily removed to a
unit, then the school will be relieved of pressure.
But if this pressure were not removed, it may be that
the school would gradually have adapted its rules,
curriculum, and teaching style, so that they became
more appropriate to the needs of the pupils. Such an
adaptation would probably be to the benefit of all
children in a school, not only those who tend to engage in disruptive activity. It should be added that
even the segregation of pupils labelled as disruptive appears to offer little help to some schools:
one ILEA secondary headteacher has been quoted as
saying,

> We have so many difficult and demanding pupils
> that we need many more such centres if we are
> to avoid suspension and exclusion of alien-
> ated, violent pupils. The internal centres
> have always helped with the management of some
> pupils, but they can only deal with a relati-
> vely small number of pupils needing help.
> (Mortimore, P. et al., 1983, p.104).

Rather than try to adapt to the needs and interests of their pupils, it is apparent that certain schools would prefer to exclude them in ever-increasing numbers.

The creation of the units may actually have inhibited the schools' ability to adapt, by draining them of a particular type of teacher. Many of the staff who work in units have been dissatisfied with the constraints of urban schools. They may have had committed and exciting ideas about what urban schools could achieve. (The high number of unit teachers who have belonged to the London Educational Alternative Project, for instance, might seem to indicate this.) They were probably those teachers, who through skill and sympathy were able to deal with disruptive situations in mainstream schools. In leaving the mainstream these teachers may have relieved it of pressure to change. Furthermore, the schools will be less capable of dealing with disruptive behaviour, since they have lost the teachers who had the skills and flexibility in this area.

1.5.3 <u>The role of segregation in education and society.</u> The children sent to disruptive units, like those sent to ESN (M) schools, and schools for the maladjusted, are not drawn representatively from all sections of society. The large-scale ILEA research makes this very clear:

> Pupils with parents in semi-skilled and unskilled occupations were over-represented among centre pupils, while pupils with parents in non-manual or skilled occupations were under-represented (Mortimore, P. et al., 1983, p.48).

Furthermore, over a quarter of the pupils' parents were unemployed as against 16 per cent at that time unemployed throughout the ILEA area. The study also indicates the over-representation of children from West Indian families placed in units, and this despite the ILEA's proclaimed initiatives on equality and race, and despite racial admission quotas at some units (p.47). Research on children referred to ESN (M) schools in Birmingham also indicated that they came overwhelmingly from working-class families, and that there was a serious over-representation of black children (Tomlinson, S., 1981). In brief, these special schools and units are for other people's children. White middle-class teachers and administrators would never expect, or accept, that their own children should be provided with such inferior and segregated education.

The special schools and units are part of "the new tripartite system" (Tomlinson, S., 1981), whereby rich parents send their children to independent schools, the mass of pupils attend mainstream schools, and many of the children of the least priviledged are sent to the bottom of the heap special schools and units. These three layers of schooling lead to three different degrees of examination success and, thus, to three different levels of employment opportunity and social position. Special schools and units are one of the institutional mechanisms whereby social stratification is reproduced through education.

A further and related role of segregation is that of social control. The units and schools are designed to control those pupils who challenge the disciplinary structures of mainstream schools. If the view of classroom disruption as a form, no matter how inarticulate, of resistant activity is accepted, then the establishment of the units provided schools with a new mechanism to overcome this resistance. The extent of the control thought necessary over some children is symbolised by the locked doors of the classrooms of some schools for the maladjusted. The doors, that is, are locked during the lesson time to keep the children inside, not during break times to keep them out. As mentioned above, the special schools and units serve also to control those pupils who are not segregated. The existence of the segregated provision is a tangible threat to all pupils of the price of non-conformity.

Finally, one of the effects of segregation is to make acceptable the ideologies of the education system (these are discussed in Section 1.6 below). These ideologies share a tendency to blame the victim. Underpriviledged children who do not thrive in school, those whom teachers fail to teach to read and write, those who refuse to conform to the often arbitrary restrictions of the system, are labelled disruptive or subnormal and excluded. The ideology behind this is that it is the pupils' own fault, and that the schools and teachers do not need to change. By making the institutional provision whereby these pupils could be segregated, the formation of the special schools and units substantiated this ideology. Teachers are able to see children as the source of difficulties and as targets for change rather than schools, curricula or pedagogical styles. Indeed, they can continue to see the educational system as helping these children, since it goes to the

expense of making segregated provison where they can
be taught by the appropriate specialists. The ideology of a munificent system and problem pupils is
sustained.

1.6 The Legitimations of the Creation of the Category.

By legitimation, we mean those beliefs whereby most
of the participants in the segregation of pupils
perceived to be disruptive can conceptualise the
process as being beneficial for everyone concerned,
and commensurate with their wider ideas about education. These legitimations include educational psychology, the practice of special education, the professionalisation of teachers in disruptive units,
and the status of academic achievement. We will discuss these issues in turn.

We will focus on two main concepts of educational psychology - intelligence and behaviour - which
serve as important legitimations to the creation of
the category.

The notion of intelligence centres on the idea
that there is one human capacity that is used to
carry out a wide range of mental tasks, and that
this capacity is differentially distributed. Beyond
this notion, the interpretation of psychological
theories deriving from studies which measure intelligence by IQ tests, has produced a whole sequence
of pseudo-scientific assertions, such as that intelligence is largely genetically transmitted, and that
it is possessed, on average, in a greater degree
by white people than by black. Both these assertions, and the notion of intelligence that underlies
them, have been questioned (Kamin, L., 1974). In
October, 1979, Judge Peckham ruled against the Cali-
fornian education authories:

> defendants have utilised standardised intelli-
> gence tests that are racially and culturally
> biased, have a discriminatory impact against
> black children, and have not been validated
> for the purpose of essentially permanent
> placements of black children into education-
> ally dead-end, isolated, and stigmatising
> classes for the so-called educable mentally-
> retarded (Evans, B., and Waites, W., 1981,
> p.10).

In England and Wales, educational psychologists have
some way to go to convince public opinion that IQ

tests are not still used for precisely this purpose.

The controversy concerning the notion of intelligence needs to be examined in greater detail than there is space for here (see Stott, D.H., 1983). Intelligence remains a major legitimation for many school practices such as eleven-plus selection and streaming, as well as for special school segregation. However, psychologists have suggested that the whole notion of intelligence may need to be abandoned, that it is not necessary to conceptualise a general mental capacity. A more parsimonious account would concentrate on the different skills which people perform. Some children, and adults, perform some tasks better than do others, whilst these other people may perform better at different tasks. Those who do not perform a task well may be taught the skill, and thus enhance their performance. The task of schools and teachers then becomes that of developing skills in pupils, rather than condemning them on a perceived lack of "intelligence". If a pupil cannot perform a task, it is precisely the teacher's job to help him/her to succeed. Lack of success might more rationally lead to condemnation of the teacher than the pupil. In practice, however, it is too often the pupils who are labelled, streamed down, or offered restricted curricular opportunities. The notion of intelligence and the commensurate practices serve both to facilitate actual classroom disruption, and to reify social judgements about it into institutional categories. It may be that the notion of intelligence and the charade of IQ testing help not the individual needs of children, but the continuation of a limited competence, flexibility and tolerance on the part of schools and teachers.

The second conception derived from educational psychology - that of behaviour - is relevant both to the definition of classroom disruption and to the categories disruptive and maladjusted. Both behavioural and psychodynamic orientations within educational psychology have developed "explanations" of disruption and maladjustment which focus on the individual child and his/her family. Difficulties in school behaviour were seen to derive from lack of discipline at home, or perhaps from too much discipline. The difficulty was seen to emanate from the social relation of the family: perhaps the child had been rejected by his/her mother, or perhaps the parents had split up and there was no father ("-figure") around. The school difficulty was thus centred firmly on the child and the family, and there was no reason for schools and teachers to examine their own practices. Casting aspersions on a child's adjustment or the stability of his/her family became for teachers an easy alternative to providing an appropriate and stimulating educational programme. Psychologists and their theories seemed to be legitimising middle-class teachers in their criticism of working-class family patterns and practices, rather than encouraging them to use these as starting points for their curriculum and pedagogy. Further, these individual-centred explanations developed in educational psychology used the criterion of behaviour as a legitimation for separate and stigmatised educational provision. Since educational psychologists legitimated this by their part in recommending pupils to provision for the maladjusted, they helped establish the educational practices and terminology within which the further category of disruptive could be discovered.

The practice of special education, indeed, constitutes a second legitimation for creating the category. We have insisted throughout this chapter on the close connection between various forms of special schools (ESN [M] and maladjusted) and disruptive units. The practices of special education facilitated the creation of the category by providing an accepted precedent for the development of categorisations. (Paradoxically, the need for the new category may have arisen when teachers and heads determined that special schools, despite their dramatic expansion, were not removing from the mainstream sufficient of those children whom they perceived to be a problem.) Special schools give institutional validity to those ideologies of intelligence and behaviour mentioned above. The existence of institutions which categorise and segregate children on a semi-permanent, usually full-time, basis exclusively on the grounds of their perceived performance and/or behaviour, provided a precedent and a model for the units. The procedures of referral and assessment adopted by many units, for instance, may be seen as the diluted version of the procedures used in special educational placement.

Similarly, the specialisation of expertise and professionalisation of teachers in special schools is a pattern which may be adopted by those working in units. Indeed, the units probably function to segregate teachers as much as pupils. Teachers who have developed skills to minimise disruption, instead of having the opportunity to transmit their expertise to other mainstream teachers by training and example, may be institutionally separated from them. Some tea-

chers in the units may not have these skills, being
attracted to the separate provision rather by dissa-
tisfaction with mainstream schools, or a vision of
alternative education. For those teachers in units
who do not possess the appropriate skills, there is,
as yet, little training, specialised help, or supervision. The absence of headteacher or hierarchical
structure limits the experience of potential em-
ployees, prevents the development of positions of
responsibility, and inhibits opportunities for promotion. Many unit teachers without adequate training,
professional support, or varied resources, yet dealing with children selected for their potentiality to
disrupt, may perhaps be in as undesirable a position
as their pupils. There are, however, indications that
professionalisation is beginning to develop among
this group of teachers. The ILEA employs an advisory
head for its disruptive pupils programme, and organ-
ises courses for the benefit of teachers involved.
Nationally, the development of NOISE (National Organisation for Institutions in Social Education) gives
further institutional validity to the units and to
the creation of the category. If this group of teachers becomes further professionalised, if the units
become acceptable educational institutions (and some
can justly claim to provide as good an education as
some schools), then the category of the disruptive
child will be further hardened by the commitment to
it of teachers' expertise and career prospects. Sad-
ly, the enhanced professionalisation of teachers
working in units may serve only to increase the likelihood of the creation of "disruptive pupils".
What, after all, is the purpose of having special
units and specifically skilled teachers if disruptive pupils cannot be found for them to remedy or
contain?

Our fourth and final element which serves to legitimate the creation of the category is the wide
concern with academic achievement in both schools
and society as a whole. It is linked to the notion
of differential intelligence discussed above. The
competitive public examination system crystallises
academic achievement and perceived "intelligence"
into certificates. Certification is one of the mechanisms whereby the rigid social stratification in
the UK has been reproduced (Halsey, A.H. et al.,
1980). In secondary schools, great importance is attached to courses leading to certification or accre-
ditation. The scrutiny devoted to a school's examination results, particularly to passes at GCE, indicates that this is a major criterion for many pa-

rents in their selection of a school. Factors within a school which militate against academic progress as conceived within these narrow terms of certification are likely to be viewed unfavourably. These factors are actually those pupils who progress slowly at schoolwork, or whose behaviour is perceived as disrupting the course of lessons.Schools, following established social values and the preference of parents, conceive their role to be the education of those who can benefit from lessons which lead to certification. Those who cannot benefit from education thus restrictively defined are therefore undesirable. The very stress on standards and the achievement of excellence for one section of the school population serves to increase the likelihood of the creation, in another sector, of disruptive pupils.

Not quite a legitimation of the creation of the category, but an excuse for the existence of disruptive units sometimes to be found in the literature (Mortimore, P. et al., 1983) is that the children are "happier" in them than they had previously been in school. From experience, too, we know of children who have indeed settled into segregated provision and blossomed there in a way which they had not done in primary or secondary school. This might be seen rather as an argument for mainstream schools to adapt to meet the needs of all their pupils rather than for the increasing proliferation of segregated provision. It is difficult to imagine that the pupils'"happiness" will continue long when the time comes for examination results and finding a job or a place at college. The ILEA research unfortunately failed to include a major category in its evaluation of the "disruptive pupils programme": it did not ask for the views of parents concerning their children's referral. In Haringey, black parents' pressure groups successfully resisted the formation of disruptive units. The parents expected more of the local education authority than that it should keep their children happy.

1.7 The Least Restrictive Environment.

It is doubtless by now apparent that we are in favour of integrating children perceived to have special needs: that is, that the widest range of children classified as having special needs should have the fullest educational and institutional integration at the earliest possible opportunity. We consider such a policy to be to the advantage of all pupils. The Warnock Report (DES, 1978) timidly en-

dorsed such a policy. It has recently been given le-
gislative and political endorsement by the 1981 Education Act and Circular 1/83. Yet, at the same time
as there are tentative moves towards integration,
the local education authorities have actually been
intensifying segregation by the invention and insti-
tutionalisation of the new category "disruptive".
Children who engage in disruptive behaviour probably
pose the greatest challenge for integration in the
schools of England and Wales. In the case of other
pupils, perceived as having special educational
needs, it is often a matter of establishing the appropriate provision in mainstream schools in terms
of equipment, architecture, ancillary help, and
skilled teachers. This calls for some administrative
energy, and the willingness to change some previously accepted perception, but otherwise it is entirely
practicable. Children who engage in disruptive behaviour are seen as jeopardising not only their own
education, but that of other pupils. Yet, as we have
suggested, disruptive behaviour in schools is best
understood in the context of schools themselves and
strategies for diminishing its incidence might again
benefit not only the labelled individuals but all
pupils.

The task of integrating children with special
needs has been undertaken in countries such as Nor-
way, the USA and Italy. Some insight might be gained
by a brief reference to the American experience. In
the USA integration is known as mainstreaming. All
children with special needs must be educated in the
least restrictive environment, that is, the context
in which their curriculum, teaching and social contacts are as close as possible to those experienced
by pupils in mainstream schools. Parents have extensive rights over the assessment and placement of
their children: they can be present at all case discussions, have access to all written material, and
can play a decisive part in determining the nature
of the educational programme. Each child who is
assessed as having special needs has an individual
education programme drawn up to ensure that these
needs are, as far as possible, being met. These programmes are reviewed annually. Of course such an ambitious policy has not been without its bureaucratic
difficulties, but it represents a national commitment that children perceived as having special needs
should not suffer educationally, or be unnecessarily
stigmatised or segregated.

By contrast, the 1981 Act does not make integration compulsory: it is only enabling legislation.

Further, the federal law in the USA provided funding for mainstreaming, but this is specifically ruled
out in the UK. Yet, much is being done in England
and Wales by committed teachers, schools, and local
education authorities to progress towards integration (Booth, T. and Potts, P., eds., 1983). In Scot-
land, progress in many areas has been more rapid,
encouraged by initiatives from HMI.

The work described and evaluated in ensuing
chapters was an attempt to reverse the movement begun in the invention of the category disruptive. It
concerned the development of strategies for helping
pupils perceived by the teachers to be disruptive to
remain in their primary and secondary classrooms.
It could be seen as part of the many projects and
initiatives which began the process of integrating
children perceived to have special needs. It dealt,
however, with perhaps the most contentious aspect
of this process, the integration of children perceived to be disruptive in inner city multi-cultural
schools. Integration took the crucial form of trying
not to remove children from school in the first
place.

The areas of theory and knowledge which supported our innovation were drawn from social psychology, organisation management theory, and social
learning theory. Further aspects of these bodies of
knowledge will emerge in the course of the book,
though they are not treated systematically. It
should perhaps be emphasised that the commitment of
the Schools Support Unit was not to the therapeutic
validity of any sociological or psychological theory, but rather to the efficacy of education itself.
In this sense, mainstream education was not only
the goal for pupils perceived as disruptive, it was
also the "treatment". The Unit suggested that good
education geared to a pupil's needs and interests
might in itself reduce disruptive activity in classrooms.

Chapter 2

A MODEL OF WORK OF A SCHOOLS SUPPORT TEAM

2.1 Responding to Schools.

The model of working we shall describe and illustrate in this chapter evolved quite quickly in Jan-
uary 1979 when the team was set up. It has been developed and elaborated since then. At the outset of
the team's work, two important internal procedures
were established: the in-depth evaluation of the
project (described in Chapter 3), and the schemes
for induction, in-service training, and consultation. In describing the model of work of the team
it is important to link it to these two procedures.
       The task initially faced by the team was how to
respond to schools when they called in a team teacher and presented him/her with a child considered
to be disruptive. Along with the child came a whole
catalogue of information about his/her behaviour,
interests, attainments, past history, and personal
and family life. Sometimes this information was on
record, sometimes it was one teacher's personal
knowledge derived from long experience, sometimes
anecdote or hearsay. The difficulty was to work out
which information was relevant and to whom.
       Having obtained information, further questions
again concerned how to respond. Should the team encourage the tendency on the part of schools to refer
individual pupils when that might simply result in
labelling the child and making the situation more intractable, especially if the difficulty is not with
the child, but with the group, the curriculum, the
teacher, the school organisation, the family, or a
combination of these? Does the presence of a Support
Team encourage schools to refer difficulties which
may go away, or diminish, if ignored, or become insignificant if the school could focus on more positive aspects of its functioning? On the other hand,

when referring a pupil, a school is often not just
acknowledging a bad state of affairs, but a worsening one, because it will have tried to improve it,
using its own resources, and failed. Thus, for a
team teacher to prevent something getting worse is
often an achievement, whereas a school may only
start to recognise success when the disruptive behaviour begins to decline in frequency.

At the same time as trying to understand these
dilemmas, there were immediate and more pressing demands to respond to. What to do about Peter, aged
fifteen, who had broken the plate-glass front doors
of his school in a rage? about Michelle, aged ten,
who monopolised teachers' attention by her complaints
about other pupils and untimely requests for help
with her work? about Richard, aged thirteen, who tended to manipulate other pupils into disruptive situations, but who would relate events at school to
his mother in such a way that she would berate the
head of year the next day?

In order to respond in a systematic way to such
pressures, and to develop a scheme of work which was
not centred exclusively on "disruptive children",
the team adopted a five-stage model of working. The
five stages are referral, assessment, formulation,
intervention and evaluation. This chapter looks at
each of these procedures in turn, and then describes
the training and supervision of the team teachers.
The procedures will be illustrated by reference to
the case of Jason, the assessment of whom was considered in the illustrative material of Chapter 1. The
first piece of illustrative material, however, consists simply of the objectives which the Support
Team set for itself early in 1979: we state them as
they were drawn up then, without the modification of
hindsight.

As these procedures and objectives were being
developed, the team was building up to its full
strength of a teacher-in-charge, twelve scale three
teachers, an educational psychologist, a clerical
officer, and a senior educational welfare officer.
They were responsible for accepting referrals from
all the primary schools - about eighty - and all the
secondary schools - about fifteen - in a borough in
the East of London. One teacher was committed to
running a small class of secondary pupils at the
team's base. Pupils attended this class only on a
part-time basis, and only for short periods. Usually
there would be about six pupils in the class, attending for periods ranging from a fortnight to half
a term. This resource provided not only a way of re-

solving crises, but also a facility whereby specific
curricular or counselling work could be done with
individual children. Pupils never attend the class
without an agreed date of full-time return to their
mainstream schools. Although the other members of
the team all had some contact with this small class,
the bulk of their work was done in the schools themselves.

2.2 Illustrative Material: The Objectives of the Schools Support Team.

The seven objectives listed below are by no means of
equal importance; the first three are of predominant
concern, and are closely interrelated.

1. To plan and implement interventions with referred
   children in terms of behavioural change, educational and curricular provision, and developmental
   progress in order to minister fully, with the collaboration of other relevant agencies, to their
   individual needs.

2. In consultation with school staff, to plan and implement interventions to educate referred children so that they benefit to the best of their ability from mainstream education and contact with
   their full peer-group.

3. By focusing on the referred child in the classroom context to prevent undue disruption to the
   education of the majority of children in the referring schools.

4. To develop skills in teachers which enable them
   to manage disruptive behaviour in a positive,
   flexible manner.

5. Through casework, to assist the development of
   school organisations capable of ministering, with
   the help of all available agencies, to the needs
   of children and their families.

6. To train and develop skills in team teachers, so
   that they are capable of undertaking their ar-
   duous and demanding job and, eventually, of
   taking posts of further responsibility.

7. To develop, evaluate and report on theoretical
   and practical approaches to disruption which may
   be of interest to others in the ILEA.

In order to correct the impression that these aims
seem rather pharaonic, it ought perhaps to be

stressed that the focus of the team's work is almost always the referred child (Coulby, D., and Harper, T., 1982, pp. 3-4).

2.3 Referral.

Referral is from a head-teacher or, in secondary school, a delegated senior teacher, to the teacher-in-charge. It involves the completion of a brief form (see illustrative material 2.4 below) containing details of the pupil's name, date of birth, address, reason for referral, whether the problem behaviour occurs more at certain times, or in certain subjects, and whether the school has discussed the referral with the parents. The advantage of the form is firstly that it provides some basic data, and secondly that it indicates some commitment by the school to the seriousness of the difficulty. Some minimal consultation between teachers in a school is ensured by having the signature of the class teacher in the primary school, and the head of year/house in a secondary school, as well as that of the head.

2.4 Illustrative Material: Referral Form on Jason.

REFERRAL FORM.

Returnable to: Schools Support Unit

Teacher-in-Charge:

Name of School: Primary

Name of Pupil: Jason

Date of Birth:

Address:

Home Tel. No.:

School Year: 1st year junior

House (if applicable):

Brief statement of reasons for referral.
Rudeness to adults. Asocial behaviour in class and
especially in playground.

Has the pupil ever attended a special school or unit?

If so, which one? No

Have any agencies been involved?

If so, which?   No

Has any other referral been made?

If so, to whom?   No

Have parents been informed of this referral?   Yes

Is the pupil's behaviour disruptive in specific lessons, situations or groups?

In a small group usually co-operative and non-disruptive. Mainly in the morning disruptive.

Recommended by: _____   (Teacher/s who asked for
                               pupil to be referred)

Signature: _____   (Head/Deputy)

                                        Date: _____

2.5 Assessment.

Assessment is the next stage and, together with the
third stage, formulation, it is usually summarised
in writing on a form. This form was originally meant
for internal use within the team to help in consultations. As the team's processes became more explicit
to schools, some teachers in schools have shared in
the completion of the assessment and formulation
form in collaboration with the team teacher. Some
schools have begun to modify the form for their own
use. Where the parents, as well as the child and the
teachers, have a distinct part to play in a programme of change, there would be every reason to
share this process with them.

Assessment involves the collection of as much
potentially relevant information as possible, eliciting some of it by standardised questionnaires, and
analysing it in a way which is helpful. Where a team
teacher visits a school regularly, she/he will probably be involved in preliminary discussions and decisions about whether or not a pupil should be referred, and so some information will already be
known prior to the completion of the referral form.
Assessment takes these informal discussions forward
to some purposeful and systematic attempts to analyse the difficulty. Perhaps the most important element in this is commitment on the part of the team
teacher and school teachers. The school teacher is
asked to complete two questionnaires, whilst the
team teacher commits time, usually to observing the
class (though only, of course, with the consent and
co-operation of the teachers involved).

2.5.1 Use of questionnaires. The two questionnaires
involved are the Bristol Social Adjustment
Guide (BSAG) (Stott, D.H., 1974), and a Behaviour
Checklist devised by the team at the outset of their
work. Their general use and limitation is discussed
at greater length in Chapter 3. Between them, they
give a fairly comprehensive picture of a child's
behaviour as seen by a teacher in the classroom and
around the school.

The BSAG asks the teacher to underline statements about a child's behaviour in the classroom -
responses to the teacher, to other children, to work
demands - at play, and in informal social situations,
and also about the child's personal ways - tidiness,
presentation, bodily mannerisms. For a teacher familiar with the questionnaire and the child, it takes
about fifteen minutes to complete. It has the advan-

tage of asking the teacher to think about the child in many situations, and not just about his/her problem behaviour. From the results of the BSAG it may emerge that the problems are more general than the referred disruptive behaviour, or that there are others which are more salient than those previously mentioned by teachers. It may emerge that a few inappropriate behaviours are quite specific, and that in many other ways the child is behaving positively in social contexts. The BSAG can be scored to compare the child with a standardised sample across England and Wales and, now that it has been completed on many children in the locality, these scores are also available for comparison (see Chapter 3). The scores are a helpful guideline to the severity of a problem. Moreover, the team has found that certain patterns of behaviour around school are characteristic of certain ages, and that some patterns are more intractable than others. Like all standardised instruments, the BSAG has its limitations, but when one learns to work within those, and not to overinterpret, then familiarity with it helps to find in it one's own yardsticks and warning signals.

Compared with the generality of the scope of the BSAG, the Behaviour Checklist is very specific. The former allows a loosening of the reasons for referral, the latter demands a tightening. The Checklist is a list of 119 behaviours which are potentially disruptive in the classroom. It is worth recalling at this point the cautions emphasised in Chapter 1: disruption is the product of a school context in which the pupil is only one of the participants. The BSAG and the Checklist provide indications only of teachers' perceptions of pupils' behaviour. They are not to be used as if they somehow measured the child and provided some indication of how "disruptive" she/he is. Disruption is a relative phenomenon. What one teacher may understand as disruption may be totally unremarkable. Similarly, different schools have different rules, and so behaviour can come to have very different meanings. For example, calling out to the teacher may by quite normal in one class/ school, whereas in another it would be considered as most disruptive and worthy of summary action. This can become obvious when pupils transfer from one school to another, or even when they change classes within a school. Therefore, in designing a checklist of potentially disruptive behaviour, it would have been misleading simply to have a list ticked for whether a given behaviour was shown by that pupil or not. Some indication of frequency was also needed.

But, without doing a series of controlled observations,it was not possible to establish absolute frequencies of a behaviour. Therefore it was necessary
to ask the teacher to make a judgement of how frequent the behaviour was relative to other pupils. A
three-point rating was used: 0 for as frequent as
an average pupil; 1 more frequent than average; 2
much more frequent than average. This relative judgement had the advantage, by reference to the behaviour
of other pupils, of taking context into account to
some extent. One further rating category was needed
to allow for either gross differences between schools
or the fact that a certain behaviour is just inapplicable to certain ages. That is to say that some
behaviours on the list may not apply to any child in
the class or school. In such cases the teacher was
provided with a category 'nn' (inapplicable) to tick.
   The Behaviour Checklist thus presents the team
teacher with a great deal of information - 119 potentially disruptive classroom behaviours rated as
0, 1 or 2. Also, space is left for the school teacher to add any other behaviour and rate it. Finally, the Checklist asks the school teacher to list
the five most disruptive behaviours shown by the referred pupil and estimate their absolute frequency
per lesson, day, or week, whichever applies. Despite
its rather negative tone, then, the Checklist has
proved to have extensive practical worth.
   But these two instruments do not comprise the
whole assessment. These questionnaires are very much
child-centred, whereas the model of disruption adopted by the unit is context-centred. It is necessary,
then, to supplement the picture shown from the BSAG
and the Checklist. One method of coming to a more
balanced picture is by classroom observation.

2.5.2 <u>Classroom Observation.</u> Observation of human
       activity, when the subjects are aware of the
observer, is not an entirely objective process. The
behaviour of the subjects is likely to be affected
by the presence of the observer, and the picture obtained thus distorted in some ways. But the reciprocal nature of such observation does provide a potential focus for growth and change, given integrity
and tact. In order for an observation to be accurate,
the observer would have to use a one-way screen or
hidden cameras, and observe over a long period of
time under different conditions. This would be im-
practical and ethically very dubious. Furthermore,
what is the purpose of attempting such accuracy? Indeed, why is classroom observation important? It

gains first-hand experience of the context (in this
case the classroom) in which it is hoped that changes will take place to everyone's benefit. It provides information, recorded both objectively and sub-
jectively, about the frequency and importance of behaviour. The crucial point is that this can be compared with similar information gathered again when
attempts at change have taken place. Certainly, the
effect of the presence of an observer is likely to
make this information skewed. But this does not entirely invalidate it, since the re-observation is
likely to be skewed in a similar way and, therefore,
the two results are comparable.

But a further purpose of observation is more
than simply to provide information which can be compared across time. Feedback of observation information to the participants is a necessary part of the
process. It can be very threatening for a teacher
and, indeed, for pupils, to have someone sitting si-
lently in their classroom, watching them and taking
notes. It is helpful to speak to the class teacher
immediately after the lesson, feed back an account
of what was observed, show him/her the notes which
were taken, and use the observation as an introduction to discussing the events of the classroom in a
detailed way. Team teachers, therefore, need to develop skills in observation, but perhaps even more
important to become skilled at feedback. One result
of this process may be that class teachers may become interested in observation. They may then develop
skills of participant observation whilst they are
teaching, in order to monitor the progress of the
class, or a particular child, or group. When this
happens, there is an enhanced possibility of change
since the teacher can be encouraged to experiment
with different methods and to monitor their relative
success by means of participant observation (Berger,
M., and Wigley, V.,1980). The descriptions of observation technique which follow, however, apply to an
outside observer coming into a classroom.

The observer needs to have a system of recording which notes only what is seen and not what is in-
ferred. The BSAG, the Checklist, and the use of
classroom observation procedures are all part of an
attempt to concentrate on specific behaviours. The
reason for this is to attempt to move away from general, ascriptive descriptions of a child - disruptive, hyperactive, disturbed, aggressive, maladjusted,
deprived - towards a specific, neutral description of
what events are happening in the classroom. This movement can be seen in the illustrative material in

this and the preceding chapter. The point is that
the more general ascriptive labels imply something
wrong in the child which cannot be changed, whereas
the behaviour specific description points to specific classroom events which are a relatively conventional thing for a teacher to alter. At the end of
this process, then, teachers in the school are beginning to describe children and events in a different way. The advantage of this is not purely seman-
tic, since the new behaviour-specific way of describing events helps them to shift from an intractable
personality problem to a conventional difficulty of
classroom, or school, organisation. Inferences and
value judgements, then, should be kept to a minimum
and, if recorded, should be in such a way as to facilitate rather than inhibit subsequent discussion
with the class-teacher and perhaps the child/ren.
Feedback, as a central aspect of the observation process, is the point at which behaviour-specific descriptions can begin to be developed.

Each observation period should have a definite
purpose and a specific means of recording. These
should be discussed with the class teacher in advance, and a time for beginning and ending agreed.
The first observation may best be a general and reciprocal familiarisation: the necessity for, and
purpose of, subsequent observations would depend on
the relative complexity of events in the classroom.
Elaborate systems have been evolved by researchers
and by members of the Support Team to record observations of a whole class, of sequences of behaviour,
or of an individual pupil's interactions with others.
They are likely to be more precise if some form of
time-sampling is adopted, for example noticing exactly what is happening every tenth, thirtieth, or six-
tieth second. Simpler systems of recording may involve just a notation of whether a child is attending to the task (on-task) or not. Usually, however,
some detail of the off-task behaviour is quite easy
to record and much more informative, for example
moving, making noises, looking out of the window,
talking. When observing an individual pupil it is
sometimes a good idea to keep an eye on another of
the same sex as a crude form of comparison. Perhaps
other pupils are engaging in very similar behaviour,
but only one has been referred: this is the kind of
point which could subsequently be discussed with the
class teacher. If the observations are of a systematic nature, sheets can be drawn up in advance to
make the recording easier to enter and to analyse.

Observation, then, is a key part of the assessment procedure. It is a learning process, whereby the team teacher gains a first-hand understanding of what the teacher sees as a difficulty - looking at the frequency of the disruptive behaviour, the preceding events, the setting, the task, the subsequent events (reactions of others). All of these events are points for continuing discussion with the teacher. These discussions lead to the development of behaviour-specific descriptions and on to the stage of formulation.

2.6 Illustrative Material: Assessment Material on Jason.

The assessment of Jason was, in part, used in Chapter 1. Here we present some of the raw material on which this assessment was based.

At the time of referral, Jason scored on the BSAG as follows: Ovract 27 (1st percentile); Unract 6 (20th percentile); Inconsequence 7; Stability 13. On the Behaviour Checklist he scored 17 ones and 20 twos. His results on these questionnaires six months and twelve months after referral are presented in the evaluation section later in this chapter.

The team teacher also talked to teachers in the school as described in Chapter 1. Because of pressure to begin intervention early, and because of the attempt to involve the home in this case, the team teacher only carried out two brief observations. These, however, confirmed the class teacher's impression of Jason's classroom behaviour. The class teacher had specified as the three most serious behaviours which Jason presented: "hits children in free situations"; "hits children in playground"; "pokes children when in free activity". These were three behaviours which the class teacher wrote on the Behaviour Checklist out of a possible five. However, in the observation Jason was not noticed as being able to make contact with the other children in either a co-operative, friendly, or work-related way. The impression of isolation suggested by other teachers in the school was also confirmed.

2.7 Formulation.

The process of formulation is crystalised by the need to complete the assessment and formulation form. This form is ideally completed in conjunction with teachers in school. It is confidential and personal to those teachers, and not intended to be passed on in the pupil's records. It could, however, be helpfully made available to parents and others concerned with the pupil at the time.

The first question asks the teacher to re-state the problem in behavioural terms. The assessment process of shifting from the ascriptive language often found on referral forms to a behaviour-specific description is thereby completed.

The second question specifies the context in terms of the setting (classroom, playground, corridor, dining room), the task, the group, time of the day or week. The teacher then attempts to work out what events immediately precede the problem behaviour. The reaction of others is the next stage, and often this is divided up into the reaction of the teacher or other adults, and the reaction of other pupils. Following this, the teacher tries to establish what reinforcements maintain the behaviour. The reinforcements may vary from the teacher getting angry, the peer group laughing, avoidance of work, etc. The following section gives a completed assessment and formulation form on Jason.

Sometimes the answers to the second question alone are sufficient to understand the problem behaviour, and can provide a formulation which leads to objectives for intervention. When this is so, there is no need to consider the next section of the form on predisposing factors. These could include relevant aspects of the pupil's personal history, performance, temperament, parental attitudes or medical, linguistic or cultural circumstances. The sort of considerations which may be relevant may be traumatic personal events (accidents, loss or death of close family), or either specific or general learning difficulties. Otherwise, a child may seem almost by nature to be very restless or impulsive, or reactive to the slightest outside stimulus. This would mean, especially for younger children, that learning self-control in social situations might be difficult. Medical history may be important, or more often the reactions to medical problems such as the overprotection of an asthmatic child, or parents' perceptions that a bump on the head in a child's infancy changed his/her behaviour. School problems may be exacerbated by language difficulties, if English is not the first language, or by cultural differences between home and school. Parental attitudes to the school may overtly, or covertly, reinforce the problem behaviour. It is important to note that these may all be predisposing factors, but they are not determining ones. Not every child with a particular

personal history will exhibit the same sort of behaviour in school. Likewise, the same child may behave
differently in a different school.

Teachers often tend to assume that home factors
actually determine classroom behaviour. When they
are having difficulty with a child, they will point
to the fact that she/he has a "poor home"; that "the
father drinks a lot"; that the parents have split
up. Judgements, often class-based, about the child's
home circumstances are used as "explanations" of
classroom behaviour without any need to examine the
more immediate and obvious, but potentially more
threatening, classroom context. Once such an explanation is adopted, it also follows that there is little
that the class teacher can do to ameliorate the situation. Such explanations exonerate the school and
legitimate the teacher's feeling of despair. The
formulation attempts to get the home factors and the
school factors into a realistic perspective. Only if
elements in the classroom and school context seem
insufficient to account for the disruptive behaviour,
is it seen as necessary to examine the child's home
circumstances or personal history. Often the school
will already have some knowledge of these. Where
they are considered to be relevant, it is helpful to
discuss them with the pupils and the parents. If
this course were to be followed, it would be necessary for the school to discuss the whole issue with
the parents and obtain their consent for a team
teacher to be involved with their child on an individual basis. (Withholding consent - which has never
happened - would not preclude some involvement with
the whole class or with the teacher.)

At this stage, it is possible that more assessment material may be needed. If more information is
required about the child's functioning, the parents'
consent for assessment by an educational psychologist may be requested. If it concerns family matters,
and social or medical agencies have been involved,
the parents' consent to consult with those agencies
will need to be obtained.

Formulation is the link between assessment and
intervention. Its importance lies as much with providing that link for everyone concerned as with the
finesse of the thought processes involved. The more
that a school can be involved in the formulation,
the more committed it will be to the interventions
that follow from it. Formulation, then, is the process of drawing together the assessment into two or
three sentences to say why the disruptive behaviour
occurs. It is a working hypothesis that is to be

tested and can be revised. Some are more precise than
others, but to have one at all is better than to
operate on implicit assumptions and expectations.
The formulation will summarise what predisposes the
behaviour, what precipitates it, and what reinforces
it.

2.8 Illustrative Material: Assessment and Formulation Form on Jason.

CONFIDENTIAL

ASSESSMENT AND FORMULATION

Name of pupil: Jason   Date:

School: Primary   Team Teacher:

A. ASSESSMENT

1. Assessment made: Bristol Social Adjustment Guide ✓
   Behaviour Checklist ✓
   Classroom Observation ✓
   How many? 2
   Attainment   Tests?
   Interview pupil ✓
   Interview parents ✓
   Discussion with staff ✓
   Anything else?

2. Restatement of the problem in behavioural terms
   (Specify frequency of the behaviours and whether estimated or observed).

Does not comply with norms of ·behaviour at school
i.e. hits children, runs off, when in a group and
when unsupervised by class teacher. Pokes, hits
children when in group activity (observed 2/3
times a day). Fights, hits children in playground
(estimated 2/3 times a week).

3. Factors which trigger and maintain behaviours
   in school - State Factors -
   (i) what is the setting? (place, task, group,
   time. There may be different settings for
   different behaviours).

Class: group work, co-operation needed, i.e.
making dough, morning worse than afternoon.
Playground: lunchtimes.
   (ii) what triggers the behaviours?
'free' unstructured, situation with no/few explicit boundaries and no 1:1 attention from adult.
   (iii) what is the reaction of others?
Ignore him, excluded from peers, reported to C/T
or H/T - gentle reasoning, told off.
   (iv) what reinforcements maintain the behaviours?
Attention, exclusion from group - odd man out,
different, alone
cont'd

ASSESSMENT AND FORMULATION form - cont'd

4. Are there any historical, medical, developmental or cultural factors which may have some bearing on the child's behaviour in school? (N.B. These are only relevant if the problem cannot be formulated from information in 3 i-iv alone)

Personal history: (obtained from mother) - confused home situation, father and mother divorced, father maintains some contact with children but very 'weak' presence. Mother has new partner who is very dominant and treats mother openly as inadequate.

B. FORMULATION

1. Why do you think the problem behaviour(s) occur?
Different messages, both within home and between home and school - child confused - poor social skills with peers - wants peer approval - wants love and to be liked - has not been given the chance to learn how to obtain this.

2. What are the objectives of intervention in specific terms, not naming techniques?

- to involve mother in child's academic progress
- to support mother re her feelings of inadequacy and not coping
- to work out strategies for managing J's hitting which do not result in a great deal of adult attention, and which do not exclude him from the group for long (less than 5 minutes).

3. Do all the participants in the planned change agree on the objectives? (Pupil, teacher[s], team-teacher, parents [not necessarily involved]).

Yes.

4. If not, how would you modify the objectives in 2?

Proposed length of intervention in weeks: 6

Method of evaluating: informal monitoring observation

Review date:

2.9 Intervention.

Chapter 4 provides a detailed description of intervening in classrooms, Chapter 5 of intervening in
school organisations. This section, then, concentrates only on the way in which intervention fits into the other stages of the model. In fact, intervention often shades into assessment, since the fact of
having someone from outside examining a situation is
likely to provoke change. Hopefully, if the assessment is systematic and involves the school teachers
in the process, the initial changes will be more than
a mere placebo effect.

The difficulty comes when the initial situation
is so disrupted that it is impossible to engage in a
protracted period of assessment. It would be absurd
to go into a classroom with stopwatch and notepad if
there were regular episodes of chair-throwing, say,
or vicious bullying. In such a case some temporary
management strategy would need to be adopted. This
usually involves withdrawing the pupil from volatile
situations either to work alone or in a small, closely supervised group. (The Support Team's own class,
described in section 2.1, can sometimes be useful in
this respect, where no facilities can be provided in
school.) There are considerable risks with this kind
of peremptory intervention. If the intervention is
unsuccessful, frustration and disappointment may attend the first endeavours of the team teacher. If it
is successful, then there may be a tendency to confuse containment and management of the pupil with
actual amelioration of the whole situation. The pupil may be returned to the normal timetable and,
since neither the pupil, nor the context, has actually changed, the same, or similar, disruptive behaviour is likely to re-occur, and this time the teachers' response is likely to be less patient. There
is little point in returning a child into exactly
the same classroom context in which she/he has previously engaged in disruptive behaviour.

Thus, early intervention or short-term management of a problem, if it is essential, must be evaluated to understand the pupil's reaction in attitude as well as in behaviour. Behaviour may change
through self-restraint, or through being placed in a
different context. But self-restraint is unlikely to
last without attitude change, especially if the pupil is returned to the context in which the disruption originally occurred. The school teachers' response to early intervention also needs to be gauged.
If the intervention is due almost entirely to an

outside person, gratitude may be followed by resi-
dual feelings of resentment. Further, the school
teachers may feel some relief, but this may actually
diminish pressure on them to change to meet the pupil's needs: possibilities for change in the context
may be reduced. When engaging in immediate, short-
term interventions, then, three considerations need
to be made. Firstly, who is going to carry out the
intervention, and who is going to be seen to be responsible for it? Secondly, how long is it to last
before a review? A brief period probably needs to be
agreed by all the participants, with a firm review
date. Thirdly, what can be learnt about the pupil
and the context needs to be established, so that
this can contribute to the assessment and can effect
the planning of the longer-term interventions.

For longer-term interventions, it is possible
to draw up from the formulation some objectives relating to the predisposing factors which may (ideally) be capable of change, the precipitating factors,
and the pattern of reinforcements. It is important to
consider even ideal objectives - although changing
the council's housing policy may be a bit too hope-
ful - since they increase awareness of which systems
do actually impinge on school difficulties. If, over
a number of cases in the same school, certain systems are seen to be important in predisposing disruptive incidents, then staff may become aware that
these should be examined. In a particular case the
listing of ideal objectives helps to temper the expectations of concrete behaviour change. Once they
are listed, teachers can then discuss what, in practice, can be done.

This usually falls into four main areas. The
first is the classroom which is discussed in Chapter
4. The classroom is the main focus of the Schools
Support Team's work. The second is the individual
pupil, work with whom would involve teaching specific skills, academic or social, examining his/her
perceptions of behaviour, motivation for change, and
ways of maintaining change. The third area is whole
school organisation, which is discussed in Chapter
5. The fourth area is the home which may mean improving communications between the school and the
family. It may further involve suggesting to the parents that a referral to another service may help
with regard to certain family problems. The team's
senior educational welfare officer would usually be
closely involved in such cases.

A model of work of a schools support team

2.10 Illustrative Material: Intervention in the Case of Jason.

As is clear from section B2 of the Assessment and Formulation the case of Jason was rather different from the usual work of the team, in that it centred more on the family. It is helpful to have an illustration of a case which differs slightly from the normal approach outlined in Chapter 4, and which attempts to deal with some of the wider predisposing factors. The team teacher involved the team's senior educational welfare officer (SEWO) in work with the mother. The team teacher also tried to develop a positive relationship between mother and the school. In addition, work was undertaken with Jason in collaboration with the class teacher. The following are contacts made by the team teacher.

Team Teacher Contacts.
(These comments are chosen from specific weeks to show the pattern of contact.)

Week 1. Observation and discussion with class teacher.

Week 3. First look at Formulation - discussed importance of home factors. Arranged with head that class teacher should speak to Jason's mother.

Week 4. Discussed with class teacher. Mother had wanted to meet team teacher. Arranged this for following week.

Week 5. Team teacher meets mother, agrees need for regular support, and arranges for the team's educational social worker to visit.

Week 7. Completion of formulation.
Class teacher reports added interest by mother in Jason's progress.
Agreed school interventions with class teacher. These were also discussed with mother by educational social worker, and agreed.

Week 10. J. continues to improve. Agreed that class teacher would inform mother by letter of improvement, and that educational social worker would also mention it on next visit to mother.

2.11 Evaluation.

When the interventions have been planned and agreed,
it is necessary to establish who is going to do what,
and how and when the progress is going to be evaluated. Evaluation may be informal, and by report or
by self-(i.e. pupil) report, by questionnaires, or
by observation. Sometimes it is worth setting out in
writing the form of the evaluation, and when it will
be reviewed, so that everyone has something to which
to refer. Informal evaluation of a subjective nature
is going on all the time, and sometimes it is best
just to bring this together at a pre-arranged review. This review may also include the parents and
pupil where appropriate. It may be carried out by
separate discussions rather than a large conference.
By setting one or more review dates in advance,
and by agreeing on the means of evaluation, it may
be possible to avoid a reactive response on the part
of school teachers if, in the course of the intervention, there is a breakdown in progress. Any sud-
den change of behaviour for the worse can be inter-
preted negatively, in contrast to the non-disruptive
behaviour which the pupil has been gradually developing. Teachers may conclude that a hesitation in
progress indicates that the pupil has not really
changed and, moreover, could not. It is necessary
for the team teacher to maintain behaviour changes
with school teachers, since it is not only the pupil
who may slip back into old behaviour patterns. It
sometimes helps to explain in the first place that
slipping back is to be expected from time to time.
The setting of a fixed review date prevents any participant interpreting a hiccup as a calamity. Another value of a well-prepared review meeting is
that it allows the team teacher and the school to
look at the assessment and formulation again. The
temptation is, if progress has not been very fast,
to change the intervention. This should only be done
if a re-assessment and reformulation indicate it.
Thus, the five stages of casework - referral,
assessment, formulation, intervention, and evaluation - form at first a linear progression, but then
the evaluation may form a loop back to assessment
and formulation. As a result intervention may continue in the same or different form. Eventually, it
is a good idea to evaluate using a repeat of the
assessment questionaires, the BSAG, and the Behaviour Checklist. The scores can then be compared
with the original ones, and this can help decide
whether the involvement of the team teacher needs to

continue or not. If it is decided that the case can be closed, then the key teacher/s who have been involved with the child are also asked to rate on a five-point scale, the change in up to five problem behaviours for which the referral was originally made. The questionnaire data and the rating data are then used in the evaluation of the overall casework that is described in the next chapter.

2.12 Illustrative Material: Evaluation in the case of Jason. (Raw scores)

The intervention in the case of Jason was successful, and the case was ready to be closed at a review meeting six months after referral. The following data was obtained: BSAG and Checklists both for the review meeting, and six months after the case was closed, i.e. post-intervention rating scale. The BSAG and Checklist scores may be compared with those obtained at assessment (see tables 1 and 2).

Table 1: BSAG's on Jason.

	Ovract	%	Unract	%	Inconse-quence	Hosti-lity
Referral	27	1	6	20	7	13
6 months	20	5	4	32	5	9
12 months	18	6	4	32	5	8

Table 2: Behaviour Checklists on Jason.

	Ones	Twos
Referral	17	20
6 months later	15	6
12 months later	12	6

(See Evaluation and Review example for Post Intervention Rating.)

The results confirm the improvement in Jason's behaviour. It is revealing that the improvement was maintained after the completion of the team's involvement.

A model of work of a schools support team

EVALUATION AND REVIEW

Name of pupil: Date: 6 months after referral

School: Team teacher:

1. How was the period of intervention evaluated?
rating scale/regular informal monitoring/self-monitoring/observation/others (please specify).

    2nd BSAG and BC

2. Who was present at the review?
pupil/parents/teacher(s) (give names and positions)

    Mother, teachers - class teacher and head

3. What was the outcome?
a) Rating scale (The scale should be completed independently by school's teacher(s). Please note change in behaviour as a result of intervention. Specify up to five behaviours for which referred.

		much worse				much better
1.	hits children in 'free' situation	-2	-1	0	+1	(+2)
2.	hits children in playground	-2	-1	0	+1	(+2)
3.	pokes children when in group activity	-2	-1	0	+1	(+2)
4.		-2	-1	0	+1	+2
5.		-2	-1	0	+1	+2

b) Action (tick where appropriate)
re-assessment and reformulation
referral to another agency (please specify)
further period of same intervention (please specify length)
closure ✓

4. If closure, please complete.
closure date: returned:
date of 2nd BSAG given: given for this review
date of 2nd BC given: given for this review
date of 3rd BSAG given:
(6 months after closure)
     next September   returned October
date of 3rd BC given:
(6 months after closure)
     next September   returned October

A model of work of a schools support team

2.13 Support Team Teachers: Their Job, Training and Supervision.

The role of the team teacher as set out in the model of working above is a complex and stressful one. Some of the criteria used in appointing team teachers are mentioned in Chapter 4. Since 1979 support teams have been established in other parts of the country to work with children with special needs, or those conside- red to be disruptive. The organisation, training and supervision of these teams differ markedly. Yet, these three factors can determine the effectiveness of the entire team's work. The practice of casework, as described in the preceding sections of this chap- ter, calls for considerable abilities to analyse and to reflect, to empathise and to act, to proselytise, and to support. It demands considerable knowledge and experience of teaching and of current educatio- nal issues. Training, stimulation and support are, then, essential. By examining the practices of the Schools Support Unit, this section attempts to indicate how these can best be provided.

2.13.1. The Organisation of Team Teachers. The area
where the team works is broken up into "pat- ches". In each patch two or three team members are responsible for working in all the primary and secon- dary schools. This means that all team teachers work in both primary and secondary schools. It also means that there are usually two team teachers working in each large secondary school, so that there is the ability, if necessary, to cope with fluctuations in the number of referrals. Two teachers working toge- ther in the same school can also offer each other insight, support and advice. One team teacher is responsible for the class at the Unit, but this per- son does not spend the whole week in the class, and may retain some cases in schools. The teacher at the Unit's class changes on a termly or yearly basis, so that all members of the team remain in contact with the central aspect of their work which is located in schools. Other team teachers retain contact with the class, especially if they have pupils from "their" schools placed there, usually by offering some spe- cialist curriculum subject at some stage of the week.
        The diary of a team teacher can, then, become a matter of complexity. If the week is divided into ten half-day sessions, four may be spent working in one secondary school, three in three separate prima- ry schools, one teaching in the Unit's class, one at the case conference at the Unit (see below), and the

tenth visiting a family or contacting another agency.
Given that the four sessions in the secondary school
probably mean working with five different year heads
and at least as many pupils, and that time is also
needed for fixing appointments on the phone and for
writing letters and notes, then the complexity is increased. Furthermore, it is necessary to find time
for consultations with the educational psychologist
and the senior educational welfare officer once a
term, and with the teacher-in-charge twice a term.
It is usually difficult to have quiet conversations
with teachers during lesson time, so this involves
appointments either at lunchtime or after school.
Similarly, many families can only be contacted when
parents return from work. So, in addition to its complexity, the diary of a team teacher can also be re-
markably full.
    A main stress of the work consists in the fact
that in a school the team teacher is always an outsider on someone else's territory. Furthermore, that
territory may change two, three, or four times a day.
The stress and constraints of the work are similar
to those of a salesperson, except that the criterion
of success is far less tangible than a sale. Teachers
respond to these stresses in different ways; some
may try to become insiders in a particular school,
and be accepted as such to a degree. Others, in times
of difficulty, may withdraw slightly from contact
with schools and concentrate on "safer" activities,
such as contacting parents, teaching, liaising with
other support services, looking for a new job, or
being ill. In this busy and stressful role, team
teachers need not only training and supervision, but
support and advice. These are provided through the
processes of induction, consultation, and in-service
training.

2.13.2. <u>The Induction of New Team Teachers.</u> The de-
        tailed checklist used by new members of the
team to ensure they cover all stages of induction is
presented as illustrative material at the end of
this chapter. It indicates the range of material
which it is necessary for new team teachers to cover.

    The policy of having team teachers work in both
primary and secondary schools was deliberate. It was
hoped in this way that some of the positive strategies for preventing classroom disruption developed
in each sector may be spread to the other. Further,
it made it possible to support pupils at the point
of secondary transfer, which can often be a difficult

time. Many of the team teachers have had experience
in special education, where the primary-secondary
division is often not so hard and fast. However, the
induction procedure does attempt to take account of
the fact that new team teachers may have little experience of one of the two sectors, primary or secondary. New team teachers usually spend a week working
in the school sector with which they are unfamiliar:
that is, teachers whose main experience is in primary schools, work in a secondary and vice versa. The
schools chosen for this experience are the ones on
the "patch" which the team teacher will ultimately
be working, so this teaching experience also provides an opportunity to begin making contacts.

A new teacher has a one-term induction period
consisting of a three-week block at the start, followed by weekly two-hour sessions. Some of the team's
in-service training sessions, which all members of
the team can attend, are also geared to meeting the
needs of new teachers. Although a lot of time in the
first weeks is inevitably spent with the teacher-in-
charge and the educational psychologist, other members of the team are also involved in the induction
process. The new team member is paired with an experienced team teacher to help him/her through the
induction period. This not only promotes a less formal direction to the induction, it also helps to begin to break down the isolation felt by any newcomer
entering an established team of people. The seminar
approach is used as little as possible, and is sup-
plemented by a series of visits to other provision
in the area, and by practical work and simulation
exercises. Not all the theory can be covered in this
way, and some reading is therefore expected of new
team members. But many of the practical aspects of
a team teacher's work can be taught through role-
play sessions, using a video camera (originally pur-
chased for social skills sessions with teenagers).
A growing stock of recorded material also provides
helpful illustrative material. Role-plays may include
such topics as interviewing a recalcitrant pupil,
supporting a harassed headteacher not to give up
with a pupil, convincing a sceptical teacher that a
certain approach may be worthwhile, knowing when to
listen instead of giving ready, facile answers.

Running alongside the acquisition of knowledge
and experience during the induction period is the
gradual recognition of the models provided by other
team members for offering various forms of support.
This occurs in one-to-one sessions, in small groups,
and in the meetings of the entire team. Team teachers

find themselves in situations in school, both one-
to-one with pupil or teachers, and in groups where it
is they who are being called on for support. As an
outsider it takes time to be accepted and to make
significant contributions either in terms of inform-
ational input or professional support. Therefore,
the experience of a new team teacher becoming part
of the team, and of different groups within it, is
one that will be repeated many times in schools. The
internal processes of the unit mirror the experiences of team teachers in schools. This reflection can
also be seen in the processes of supervision and
consultation and in in-service training.

2.13.3 Inservice Training. The team's weekly in-
service training sessions last one and a half
hours. At the outset of the team's work attendance
at them was compulsory but, since some material is
inevitably repeated as new teachers join the team,
it later became voluntary. From the start the team
was committed to the importance of in-service training and especially to sharing skills among the members of the team (as they would, in turn, share them
with teachers in the schools). In designing the programme, the teacher-in-charge tries to cater for various needs expressed in the course of the previous
term.
    Topics covered include current issues in educa-
tion, such as curriculum development in maths or
anti-racist teaching, meeting special needs in ordinary schools, school organisation and management.
They also cover aspects of the psychology and sociology of education such as learning theory, delinquen-
cy, or the sociology of special education. These more
theoretical topics are introduced either by an outside speaker, or by a member of the team, who is
well-read and/or experienced in the topic.
    More practical sessions cover aspects of the
work of the team and are often grouped together in
blocks of three or four consecutive sessions. Team
teachers are then asked to commit themselves to attending all the sessions in a block. Topics covered
in this way have included interview techniques, behavioural analysis, behavioural counselling, group
work, client-centred counselling, social skills,
training and observation techniques. This type of
topic can be presented less formally through small
group discussions, role-play in small groups, video
and playback, or the use of pre-recorded video material for demonstration purposes. The programme for
a term tries to strike a balance between inside and

outside speakers, and between theoretical and practical sessions.

The aim of the in-service sessions is that they will provide material helpful to team teachers in their work in schools. Beyond this, there is also the aim of assisting the professional development of team teachers. Working in a team with so many systematic procedures ought not to inhibit the use of individual teachers' personal styles, preferred approaches, or curricular skills. The in-service training sessions provide opportunities for team teachers to widen and develop their own interests.

2.13.4 <u>Supervision and Consultation.</u> Supervision is distinguished from consultation in that the team teachers are accountable to the teacher-in-charge, who is responsible for overseeing their work and ensuring that professional standards are maintained. Supervision sessions cover all the work of a team teacher, and this ensures that every case is discussed at least twice a term. Consultation is a more open-ended process in that the consultee largely determines what is discussed. Both procedures are confidential.

Each team teacher has a two-hour supervision session with the teacher-in-charge twice a term. Before the meeting the teacher-in-charge reads the up-to-date personal notes that the team teachers keep on their work, and makes written comments. The session then usually consists of going systematically through all the cases, some faster than others. The teacher-in-charge has been observed doing this, and about a quarter of the comments are aimed at acknowledging good practice, a quarter are direct advice, and a half are joint problem-solving. As well as these two sessions a term, either the team teacher or the teacher-in-charge can request more time if necessary.

Consultation takes place three times a term with three different people, the educational psychologist, the senior educational welfare officer, and the team teacher with whom work in a particular secondary school is shared. The psychologist is also likely to look through the team teacher's notes before the session to see if there are any cases where the schools psychological service should be more directly involved. The consultation session itself, however, is for the team teacher to bring up what she/he chooses and this has included casework issues with schools or within the team, particular approaches or techniques, professional development or personal difficulties.

The consultation session with the senior educational welfare officer ensures that social work aspects of a case are covered and that, where appropriate, social work can be undertaken. The meeting with the other team teacher in the same secondary school allows them to discuss and plan their work. The opportunity to talk confidentially, particularly to the educational psychologist and the senior educational welfare officer, has provided space for team teachers to have a long-standing relationship in a job which, by its peripatetic nature, entails a great deal of fleeting, and sometimes short-term, contacts. It has also, at times, provided a valuable safety valve to air tensions within the team.

As well as these individual sessions, the team has one compulsory weekly meeting of an hour and a half to discuss cases. The format of these discussions varies between alternate weeks: one week there is a formal presentation of work on one case by a member of the team; the next week the team splits up into small groups to discuss cases in a less formal atmosphere. These discussions allow for ideas on casework and experiences in schools to be shared. They also lead to discussions about the role of the team teachers and of the team as a whole. They provide an opportunity for the team to consider the issues and cases which are of current importance. They also allow team teachers a collective voice in the direction which the work of the team ought to be taking.

There has been one aspect of the work that has provided a framework and an impetus for this structure of consultation, supervision, and training, namely the evaluation. The commitment from the outset that the work would be evaluated had profound effects: it encouraged the team to draw up precise objectives and to become aware of its own processes. It was important that the evaluation was carried out and written by members of the team - the first phase by the teacher-in-charge and the educational psychologist, and the second phase by a small working party. It was important because the feedback of results concerning the processes and outcomes of casework was compelling. Equally important was the fact that the evaluation encouraged the team to look beyond its immediate concerns, in that the intention all along was to publicise the team's work to the management committee, to schools and to anyone else interested. Details of the design and findings of the evaluation are covered in the next chapter.

A model of work of a schools support team

2.14 Illustrative Material: Induction of New Teachers.

INDUCTION SHEET

Educational

I.L.E.A.	- Green Book (Handbook of
Area Provision	Provision)
and population	- Evaluation I & II
EPA Indices	- Evaluation II R & S
Support Services	
in Area	- Booklet (Yellow)
Nursery	- Aims Practices
Primary	- " " Plowden Report
Secondary	- Hargreaves Report

Psychological

Biological Basis of Psychology
Theories of Personality
    "   of Motivation
    "   of Learning

Psychodynamic approaches)
Behavioural approaches) Experimental approaches
Systems approaches   )

Sociological

Education as Social Control - see references in
                                Evaluation I
Inequality - Jencks, Halsey, Coleman report
View of Units & 1981 Act
Urban Education - Evaluation I & II

SSU practices   Evaluation I & II
Aims
History
R.A.F.I.E. - Training. Video observation.
(Referral, Assessment, Formulation, Intervention,
 Evaluation)
Support and Supervision 1 x fortnight
Confidentiality. Records. Staff. Role of EP & EWO

SSU Administration - Criteria of note-keeping.
Paper
Travel
Communication
Developments - Special Needs, Suspensions, Evaluation
Phase III, Computerisation, Infant Project.

Chapter 3

EVALUATION OF THE WORK OF THE SUPPORT UNIT:
METHODS, OUTCOMES AND PROCESSES

3.1 The purposes of evaluation.

The illustrative material in the preceding
chapter is a paradigm for the summative evaluation
of the team. The summative evaluation is no more than
a multiple single case study design based on the
model of data collection mentioned in Chapter 2. The
exact variables on which data were collected will be
given later. Certain of these data gave useful
summative statistics in the form of means and standard deviations of variables such as age at referral,
baseline scores on standardised assessments, differences between baseline and post-intervention scores
and ratings of outcome. Frequency counts were possible
on month of referral, gender, types of intervention,
school year and school. These were helpful in planning
the allocation of resources (the time of team teachers
in different schools), and looking at referral trends
within a school and across schools. Also, knowing the
prevalence of different interventions helped in the
planning of in-service training sessions for team
teachers. These points will be elaborated in more
detail later. For the moment they serve to give an
idea of the scope of the data collection and the
practical purposes to which it has been put.
By contrast to these practical objectives, it
is important to realise that the evaluation was not
set up to answer research questions such as: - Is
one intervention more successful than any other? Is
disruptive behaviour linked to such factors as age,
gender or school year? The evaluation data may incidentally answer some of these questions, and may
point towards statistical trends. But to answer these
types of questions, especially with regard to the
effects of intervention, with any degree of confidence,
it would be necessary to have control groups and the

types of experimental conditions that are rarely possible in the day-to-day educational setting. In educational research, it is especially difficult to control intervention variables, since so many interactions take place in short periods of time. It is impossible to state without qualification that intervention 1 with teacher A in school X is comparable to intervention 1 with teacher B in school Y. For this reason, part of the evaluation design is single case studies and, by collecting data on the same variables in each case, it becomes a multiple single case design. Using this design, it is possible to say that in case A certain behavioural changes were associated with certain interventions over a certain period of time, and that these changes were or were not maintained when the interventions were withdrawn. It is also possible to say in how many cases these types of change occurred, and in how many cases other types of change could be identified.

Before proceeding to examine the precise methodology in more detail, it is important to examine the process aspect of evaluation. Evaluation is not just an assessment of systems and processes: it is a process in itself. In considering the process of evaluation, questions may arise such as: Who carries out the evaluation? Who commissions it? To what purposes is it going to be put? Who has access to any data collected? How is it going to feature in any decision making process with regard to policy or provision? The first two questions were answered explicitly at the beginning of the team's work: the teacher in charge and the educational psychologist were to carry out the evaluation at the behest of the management committee. The purposes of the evaluation were outlined in the preceding paragraphs. However, other more covert purposes might include helping to establish the identity of the team, or resolving potential disputes about its worth and its work. In these ways, the evaluation might be a source of stability. If answers to the other questions above can be found, and if the results can speak for themselves, then it may become an impetus for change.

3.2 <u>The methodology of the evaluation.</u>
The changes to be evaluated were a reflection of the objectives adopted by the team in its first year of practice (these are set out in Chapter 2). Therefore it was changes in pupils, teachers, and schools which were of interest, namely:-

1. the behaviour of pupils referred to the team;
2. the performance of other children in the class;
3. the skills and confidence of individual teachers in schools to manage disruptive behaviour;
4. the way schools as organisations conceptualise and manage disruptive behaviour;
5. the knowledge and skills of teachers in the team;
6. the use that schools make of other services.

Some of these changes are more open to quantification than others: in particular we have not yet devised a reliable way of evaluating items five and six. But other methods of evaluation, such as individual case studies, can supplement the quantified data and add flesh to the bones of numbers.

The changes do not, of course, take place in isolation from each other. One change is likely to influence another. Furthermore, the causal path of influence is not simply serial as in a chain - A influences B, and B influences A, and so on. The paths of influence are more likely to be multiple and reciprocal (see figure 3.1).

Figure 3.1.

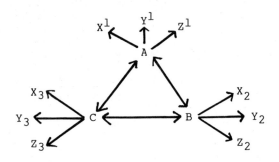

In this model the X's and Y's and Z's would also be interlinking with each other. This simple diagram contains only three main elements in interaction, but the process could involve five, six, or more. Schools are highly complex organisations, and are likely to have multiple rather than triangular interactions.

Theoretically it may be possible to change one element in a school at a time and then, by measuring consequent changes, to map its path of influence. After a number of such mappings it may be possible to determine what leads to what, and which strategies of intervention are most effective and economic using, say, cost-benefit criterion. In practice the types of intervention are not under experimental control, and several elements may simultaneously be foci of intervention. The strategy of evaluation seeks to make a virtue of necessity, by looking at the patterns of intervention and trying to find whether any systematic changes in pupil, teacher, or school behaviour occur in conjunction with these. The results of these enquiries may only point to better questions around which future evaluations might be designed.

We now take the main objectives of change in turn, explain the method of data collection, and present the results where data could be collected. Illustrative material is used to inform the numerical presentation.

3.3 The behaviour of children referred to the team.

3.3.1 Methods of data collection.

In referring an individual pupil, a teacher is suggesting that this pupil's behaviour causes difficulties to a significantly greater extent than that of other pupils. Without prolonged observation, it is impossible to determine the nature of the behaviour and the circumstances in which it arises. It is necessary to rely on the teacher's perception of the pupil's behaviour. To accept that a record of behaviour is a perception creates one difficulty and solves another. The difficulty which it creates is that if the concern is not just with the behaviour at the time of referral, but also in the change in behaviour over time, then another record of behaviour must be made after a certain period of time, possibly as short as six months. For the second record to be comparable to the first, it needs to be completed under the same sort of circumstances, and with the same sort of perceptions. Ideally, the same person would make the second record as made the first. Since this is not always possible, a safeguard is to choose a means of recording which has been shown to be reasonably reliable when used by different people. The second difficulty, which is solved, is as follows. The fact that the record may be as much of perception as of behaviour means that it might actually be a good indication of classroom disruption. As was emphasised in Chapter 1, whether a classroom activity is determined to be disruptive depends largely on the attitudes and tolerance of the teacher involved, that is on the teacher's perception of the behaviour. Disruption, then, is a construct which is a product of the behaviour, the situation, and the teacher's perception. In which case, a record of behaviour which includes these elements may be a helpful measure of disruption.

The main requirements of a record of behaviour, in summary, include: it should be as precise as possible in specifying the disruptive behaviour in a variety of school situations; it should be capable of being used reliably on a second occasion, if necessary, by a different teacher; it should be simple and quick to complete.

We found that the choice of available records was sparse, and settled for the Bristol Social Adjustment Guide (BSAG) (Stott, D.H., 1974). In addition, we developed an instrument of our own (see the description of the Behaviour Checklist below). We were aware of the limitations of the BSAG (Yule, W., 1968), and particularly that the original reliability and validity studies were not convincing. Its widespread use by the National Child Development Study had at least made it familiar to some teachers, and a degree of validity had been established in later studies (Ghodsias M., 1977). We later conducted a small reliability and validity study of our own, and concluded that the BSAG may be reasonably reliable for the same pupil across teachers, provided that they knew the pupil well (Harper, T., 1985). The BSAG had two other advantages which persuaded us to adopt it. Firstly, it had an established scoring system and so, provided that we used the raw scores and not the standard scores, we could compare the records across time and derive means and standard deviations for groups of pupils in order to carry out statistical procedures. Secondly, it contained positive, as well as negative, statements concerning a whole range of school situations. Because of this, most teachers were able to find some positive statements which applied to the referred pupil, thereby providing a more balanced account.

At this point, it would, perhaps be appropriate to describe the BSAG, and to introduce terms which will be used in describing the results later in this chapter (and which have already occurred in the illustrative material to the last chapter). The BSAG covers the following aspects of a pupil's school life: - interaction with teachers, attitudes to school work,

other children, games and play, personal ways, phy-
sique, general health and school achievement. (One
variable which it does not cover and which we omit-
ted to monitor independently was attendance.) Each
of these aspects has a set of statements which sometimes describe behaviour, sometimes interactions and
sometimes personal attitudes. The teacher is asked
to underline the statements which apply to the pupil.
The guide is then scored on two main scales: one
covers behaviour which is generally over-reactive
and so called Ovract; the other covers behaviour
which is generally under-reactive and so called
Unract. (Since we were interested in changes in perceptions, it was possible to ignore any theory behind these concepts.) Both Ovract and Unract are
divided up into sub-scales. In practice, we have
found that the two next important sub-scales, that
is those which best indicate the nature and severity
of disruptive behaviour, are two of the four scales
which comprise Ovract.These two sub-scales are called
Inconsequence and Hostility. Inconsequence includes
behaviour which seems to indicate that the pupil is
relatively unaffected by consequences (pleasant or
unpleasant). Examples of this would be: acting on
impulse, restlessness, persevering with something in
the face of pressure to stop, responding to correction
only briefly. Hostility is perhaps less neutrally defined, since it implies that, in the circumstances,
hostile reactions are not reasonable. The sub-scale
covers hostility to both peers and adults. Examples
of this would be: spoiling work on purpose, insult-
ing remarks, easily provoked into a temper, moody.
        However, we were not satisfied that the BSAG
would meet all our requirements either as an assessment instrument or for evaluation purposes. In particular, the BSAG was not specific enough in describing disruptive behaviour in the classroom, either
in its exact nature or in its frequency. We did not
find it as helpful to be informed by the BSAG that
the child was "moody" or "unconcerned about approval
or disapproval" as to know exactly what the child did,
in whose presence, and how often that prompted the
teacher to make these inferences about his/her mental
state. In order to catalogue the behaviours which lay
behind these inferences we attempted to compile a
list of behaviours about which teachers had complained.
We tried to avoid words like "aggressive", "moody",
"disobedient", "wilful", etc., but rather concentrated
on the behaviours which prompted these inferences. We
then had a list of "potentially disruptive classroom
behaviours" which we extended through discussion to

119 items. The list was then organised into categories according to whether the behaviour was movement while seated, movement while out of seat, other behaviour that could occur without involving other people except as an audience, behaviour against other pupils and, finally, behaviour against teachers. This list was called the Behaviour Checklist (see Section 3.3.2).

In order to find out about the frequency of the behaviours, we asked teachers to rate this against their idea of what they would expect of an average pupil. Thus, a zero rating would mean a usual frequency compared to what might be expected of an average pupil, a rating of one would mean more than usual, and a rating of two much more than usual. Teachers tended to make their ratings not according to some notion of a national average, nor an average of all pupils in the school, but actually according to an average for that particular class. In this case, a pupil in a difficult class might engage in disruptive behaviour, but have it only rated zero, since it was no more than average for the class. The difficulty was in deciding whether the disruptive behaviour was that of an individual, of a small group, or of the whole class. It was, therefore, found to be necessary to modify the Behaviour Checklist to include a fourth rating option for the teacher. This was 'nn' (nothing noticeable) which allowed the teacher to indicate that the behaviour in question did not apply to any pupil in the class.

The only reliability and validity study which has been conducted on the Checklist was the one mentioned above in connection with the BSAG (Harper, T., 1985). The Checklist was found to correlate significantly with classroom observation, and to be reliable across different teachers. Its validity was also strengthened by the finding that it discriminated well not only between disruptive and non-disruptive behaviour, but also between pupils who were referred because of their disruptive behaviour and those whose behaviour was disruptive but not so severe as to be referred.

A score can be derived from the Behaviour Checklists by giving two points for a behaviour rated two, and one point for a behaviour rated one, and then adding up the points. Clearly, some of the behaviours such as throwing furniture are more severely disruptive than others such as tapping a pencil. However, in scoring any behaviour one or two a teacher is indicating that its frequency is severe enough to be a problem, even though the behaviour in itself may seem innocuous.

The third means of measuring change in pupil behaviour was the first part of the Post-Intervention Questionnaire (PIQ). This questionnaire is given to the teacher in a school with whom the team has worked on a case, as soon as it has been closed. The first section deals with pupil behaviour (the other sections concerning teachers and schools are described below). The first question asks the teacher from the school to list up to five disruptive behaviours upon which work has been done, and then to rate them on a scale of minus two (much worse) to plus two (much better). Since the number of behaviours rated varied between one and five, then in order to compare outcomes on different cases or to derive average scores for groups of cases, a score had to be calculated from this first PIQ section, known as the "average behaviour rating". This was obtained for each case by adding up the ratings (e.g. +1, +1, 0, +2, -1 = 3) and dividing by the number of behaviours rated (in this example = 5) to give an average rating (= + 0.6).

The data collected on the behaviour change of individual pupils may now be summarised. At the time of referral, a teacher in a secondary school who knew the pupil well, or the class teacher in a primary school, was asked to complete a BSAG (1st BSAG) and a Behaviour Checklist (1st BC). When the case was closed, the same teacher (or if she/he no longer taught the pupil, another teacher) was asked to complete a 2nd BSAG, a 2nd BC, and a Post-Intervention Questionnaire (PIQ). Finally, a 3rd BSAG and a 3rd BC were requested at least six months after closure as a means of follow-up. Rates of return on second, and particularly third BSAG's and BC's, were, however, rather disappointing. For instance, only on the first 150 cases, for whom 2nd BSAG's and 2nd BC's were collected, did we request 3rd BSAG's and 3rd BC's. Completing questionnaires on pupils who are no longer presenting problems is clearly not rewarding, since only 58 were retrieved. The missing data open the possibility of bias in the evaluation. An attempt to check for this was made by comparing cases with missing data with cases with complete data. The data collected allowed three types of outcome scores to be computed for each pupil:-

Evaluation of the work of the Support Unit

1. differences between 1st and 2nd BSAG's
                       2nd and 3rd BSAG's
                       1st and 3rd BSAG's;

2. differences between 1st and 2nd BC's
                       2nd and 3rd BC's
                       1st and 3rd BC's;

3. average behaviour change rating from first
   section of the Post-Intervention Questionnaire.

        It should be remembered that the evaluative
model is essentially a multiple case study design.
Individual detailed case studies may arguably be as
important an aspect of evaluation of pupil behaviour
change as summative statistics, in that they provide
insights into the nature and process of change in the
sort of detail that can prove illuminating for practice. The case studies and the summative data actually
complement one another. The summative statistics
show trends and patterns which can then be highlighted
by case studies. The case studies used in this book
have been chosen to illustrate trends and patterns in
the work which the Support Team has evolved.

Evaluation of the work of the Support Unit

3.3.2 <u>Illustrative Material: The Behaviour Checklist.</u>

Schools Support Unit

<u>Checklist of potentially disruptive classroom
behaviour.</u>

This information is to help with our assessment procedure and will also form part of the data used in
the ongoing evaluation of the Schools Support Unit
project. Please circle each of the following behaviours in the appropriate column. Your decision will
depend on:
a) whether or not it is disruptive in a given
   situation;
b) the number of times you would expect an average
   child to do such a thing;
O would mean occurs a usual number of times compared
to an average pupil;
1 occurs more than a usual number of times compared
to an average pupil;
nn- please circle if this behaviour does not apply
to any pupil in the class.
Thank you very much for your co-operation.

Name of pupil: _____

			nn	O	1	2
A	1.	Turns round in seat	nn	O	1	2
	2.	Rocks in chair	nn	O	1	2
	3.	Sits out of position in seat	nn	O	1	2
	4.	Fidgets	nn	O	1	2
	5.	Plays with toys or possessions	nn	O	1	2
	6.	Shuffles chair	nn	O	1	2
	7.	Stands up	nn	O	1	2
	8.	Changes seat	nn	O	1	2
	9.	Moves from seat	nn	O	1	2
	10.	Walks about class	nn	O	1	2
	11.	Runs about class	nn	O	1	2
	12.	Leaves classroom	nn	O	1	2
	13.	Climbs on furniture	nn	O	1	2
	14.	Lies on floor	nn	O	1	2
	15.	Crawls on floor	nn	O	1	2
B	1.	Moves furniture	nn	O	1	2
	2.	Throws pellets/paper	nn	O	1	2
	3.	Throws equipment/books	nn	O	1	2
	4.	Throws furniture	nn	O	1	2
	5.	Bangs furniture	nn	O	1	2
	6.	Stamps feet	nn	O	1	2
	7.	Taps hand on furniture	nn	O	1	2
	8.	Taps pencil/ruler	nn	O	1	2

Checklist - continued

C	1. Cries	nn	O 1 2
	2. Laughs/giggles inappropriately	nn	O 1 2
	3. Makes non-verbal noises	nn	O 1 2
	4. Whistles	nn	O 1 2
	5. Sings	nn	O 1 2
	6. Tells lies	nn	O 1 2
	7. Pulls funny faces	nn	O 1 2
	8. Makes inappropriate gestures	nn	O 1 2
	9. Talks to self	nn	O 1 2
D	1. Damages own work	nn	O 1 2
	2. Damages own property	nn	O 1 2
	3. Damages class furniture	nn	O 1 2
	4. Writes on furniture	nn	O 1 2
	5. Writes on wall	nn	O 1 2
	6. Spits on floor	nn	O 1 2
	7. Deliberately disarranges dress	nn	O 1 2
	8. Hurts self	nn	O 1 2
	9. Feigns illness	nn	O 1 2
	10. Feigns need to go to the toilet	nn	O 1 2
	11. Plays with or strikes matches	nn	O 1 2
	12. Plays with or smokes cigarettes	nn	O 1 2
	13. Moves others' property	nn	O 1 2
	14. Damages others' property	nn	O 1 2
	15. Takes others' property	nn	O 1 2
	16. Interferes with teacher's property	nn	O 1 2
E	1. Carries on distracting conversation with other pupil	nn	O 1 2
	2. Shouts to other pupil	nn	O 1 2
	3. Verbally abuses other pupil	nn	O 1 2
	4. Spits at other pupil	nn	O 1 2
	5. Obliquely assaults another e.g. drawing pin on chair	nn	O 1 2
	6. Mimics other pupil	nn	O 1 2
	7. Passes food/drink to another pupil	nn	O 1 2
	8. Strikes with hand another pupil	nn	O 1 2
	9. Strikes with weapon another pupil	nn	O 1 2
	10. Pokes another pupil	nn	O 1 2
	11. Kicks another pupil	nn	O 1 2
	12. Pushes another pupil	nn	O 1 2
	13. Trips another pupil	nn	O 1 2
	14. Bites another pupil	nn	O 1 2
	15. Scratches another pupil	nn	O 1 2
	16. Pinches another pupil	nn	O 1 2
	17. "Strangles" another pupil	nn	O 1 2

Evaluation of the work of the Support Unit

Checklist - continued

			nn	O	1	2
E	18.	Clings to other pupil	nn	O	1	2
	19.	Verbally threatens other pupil	nn	O	1	2
	20.	Physically threatens other pupil	nn	O	1	2
F	1.	Fails to bring equipment	nn	O	1	2
	2.	Fails to bring correct book	nn	O	1	2
	3.	Fails to do homework	nn	O	1	2
	4.	Fails to do punishment work/ attend detention	nn	O	1	2
	5.	Carries on distracting conver- sation with teacher	nn	O	1	2
	6.	Calls out to teacher	nn	O	1	2
	7.	Shouts at teacher	nn	O	1	2
	8.	Mimics teacher	nn	O	1	2
	9.	Verbally abuses teacher under breath	nn	O	1	2
	10.	Verbally abuses teacher directly	nn	O	1	2
	11.	Clings to teacher	nn	O	1	2
	12.	Assaults teacher obliquely, e.g. practical joke	nn	O	1	2
	13.	Assaults teacher directly	nn	O	1	2
	14.	Verbally threatens teacher	nn	O	1	2
	15.	Physically threatens teacher	nn	O	1	2
	16.	Silently fails to follow teachers' instructions	nn	O	1	2
	17.	Silently refuses to attempt work	nn	O	1	2
	18.	Arrives late	nn	O	1	2
	19.	Leaves coat on	nn	O	1	2
	20.	Packs away early	nn	O	1	2
	21.	Fails to leave classroom	nn	O	1	2
	22.	Eats/drinks	nn	O	1	2

G Any other
Please specify and circle   nn O 1 2

Evaluation of the work of the Support Unit

Checklist - continued

Most disruptive behaviours.

Please list the five most disruptive behaviours -
e.g. E 16, and how often they occur.

	Behaviour	Frequency

1.   ....times per lesson/day/week*

2.   ....times per lesson/day/week*

3.   ....times per lesson/day/week*

4.   ....times per lesson/day/week*

*Please delete where appropriate and indicate whether
 this is an estimate or a direct observation.

Teacher's Name:

Date:

                              Schools Support Unit
                              November 1984.

Evaluation of the work of the Support Unit

3.3.3 <u>Results - the referral population and changes
in the behaviour of referred pupils.</u>
The Support Team works with pupils aged between 3 and
16, from nursery to the end of compulsory schooling.
The percentage of children referred at each age is
shown in Table 3.1.

Table 3.1: <u>Percentages of Children referred according to age.</u> (Jan. 1979 - Feb. 1984)

Age	3	4	5	6	7	8	9	10	11	12	13	14	15	16
% of total referrals	0.4	1.0	2.3	6.4	7.4	8.5	8.9	9.7	9.5	10.3	12.0	14.1	9.5	0.2

There have been two main changes in age distri-
bution over the five years of the Team's operation.
Firstly, the amount of work in infant schools stayed
quite low during the first two years, and then increased. The results of the first evaluation had been
made known to all the referring schools and, perhaps,
the encouraging results on infant pupils led to an
increase in referrals from that sector. Secondly, the
proportion of 14- and 15-year-olds has dropped in
relation to the 12- and 13-year-olds.
The other basic variable of the referral population is gender. The proportion of boys referred
as against girls has consistently remained 3:1 in
favour of boys. Moreover, this proportion does not
vary significantly according to age. The consistency
of this finding tallies with proportions of boys compared to girls judged by their teachers to show mal-
adaptive behaviour in the National Child Development Study (Davie, R. et al, 1972). The consistency
of this result, however, should not imply that further research is not required in the whole area of
how boys receive disproportionate amounts of teacher
attention through engaging in disruptive behaviour.
We turn now to changes in the behaviour of referred pupils. Two BSAG's were collected on 177 pupils
who were referred and worked with between September
1979 and February 1984. The work with some lasted no
longer than one term, with others it lasted up to two
years. The average length of intervention was 35

Evaluation of the work of the Support Unit

school weeks, which, if holidays are included, is approximately one year. The 1st BSAG was collected at the time of referral, and the second at the end of intervention. Table 3.2 shows the scores on those BSAG's for the two main scales (Ovract and Unract), and two sub-scales (Inconsequence and Hostility) which partly made up the Ovract score. A 3rd BSAG was collected on 58 of those cases at least six months after intervention.

Table 3.2: Mean raw scores and percentile ranks of 1st and 2nd BSAG (n=177).

	Ovract		Unract		Inconsequence		Hostility	
	raw score	%ile rank	raw score	%ile rank	raw score	%ile rank	raw score	%ile rank
1st BSAG	17.8	7th	3.3	40th	6.5	17th	5.4	6th
2nd BSAG	13.4	14th	2.3	52nd	5.4	21st	3.9	10th
Significance level of difference	<.01		<.01		<.01		<.01	

Note. Raw scores are given to one decimal place in all tables, percentile ranks are taken from Stott, D.H., 1974.

Table 3.3. shows the scores on the 2nd and 3rd BSAG's in a similar manner to table 3.2. The important point to bear in mind is that a difference in scores reflects a change in the type of statements that are underlined by a teacher with respect to the pupil. Since some of these statements, as indicated above, can cover quite general aspects of behaviour, then a small difference in score may represent quite a substantial change in the teacher's perception of the behaviour change.

Table 3.3: Mean scores and percentile ranks of 2nd and 3rd BSAG's (n=58).

	Ovract		Unract		Inconsequence		Hostility	
	raw score	%ile rank	raw score	%ile rank	raw score	%ile rank	raw score	%ile rank
2nd BSAG	15.3	10th	2.5	52nd	5.1	21st	5.1	6th
3rd BSAG	13.4	14th	2.1	52nd	4.6	28th	4.6	9th
Significance level of difference	NS	–	NS	–	NS	–	NS	–

A significant change evidently takes place in the teacher's perception of pupil behaviour between the time of referral and the end of intervention. This change takes place on the four scales of the BSAG. It should be noted that the severity of the under-reactive behaviour is not as great as for the other scales, according to the percentile ranks. The scores also show that the behaviour at the end of intervention (2nd BSAG) is not perceived to be ange- lic, that is with very low scores, but rather it re- presents a level with which the teachers in school feel they can cope, otherwise they would presumably not have agreed to the ending of the intervention. Indeed, the scores from Table 3.3 suggest that, after the end of intervention, the class teachers can do more than cope. They can actually prevent the beha- viour from worsening and, in some cases, of course, the behaviour continues to become more acceptable. The slowing down or, in the majority of the 58 cases with 3rd BSAG's, the flattening out of the rate of behaviour change gives some evidence that the change between the 1st and 2nd BSAG is a result of inter- vention, and not just an effect of the passage of time, or the maturation of the pupil.

It would be wrong, however, to expect the rate of behaviour change to be smooth. Our impression is that initial change is difficult to achieve, since the team teacher is usually called into a worsening situation. Stopping the slide can be an achievement in itself. Achieving change in a desired direction is another step. Once some change has started, fur- ther progress may actually be easier to achieve, but then there may be setbacks as this often necessitates changes in the behaviour of the rest of the class or of the teacher. If this happens, the pace of change may accelerate again, until all parties concerned (pupil, peer group, teacher) find one another's behaviour more or less acceptable. At this stage, the motivation and the space for further change is reduced to the extent that the rate of change flattens out. This pattern is illustrated in the case studies below.

Turning to the results of the Behaviour Checklists, Table 3.4 shows that the behaviour as rated on these improved in its average by a factor of more than one third.

Table 3.4: Mean scores on 1st and 2nd Behaviour Checklists (n=175).

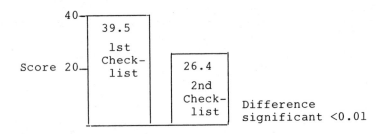

Table 3.5: Mean scores on 2nd and 3rd Behaviour Checklists (n=58).

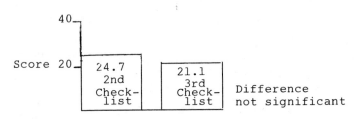

When the pattern of scoring is analysed in terms of the shift in the numbers of 2's and 1's between the Checklists, it is clear that approximately the same number of ones are scored on the first and second Checklists. The difference is that some of the 2's become 1's and some of the 1's become 0's. In other words, some of the behaviours which were rated as occurring much more frequently than average (2)

did not reduce right down to an average level (0), but, more frequently, to a more than average level (1). Since the Checklist refers specifically to observable classroom behaviours, then the significant reduction in the scores represents less behaviour that is potentially disruptive, and a classroom in which the flow of the lesson is interrupted less. Furthermore, Table 3.5 suggests that this change is maintained after the end of the intervention, since the 3rd BC was collected at least six months later. As with the BSAG scores, this flattening out of the rate of reduction is a strong argument for the existence of a true intervention effect: the change seems to be due to the intervention and not to chance factors, or simply the passage of time. It is encouraging, however, that the reduction is maintained after the end of intervention, even though the reduction does slow down. Thus, intervention is not just like putting a finger in the dyke. It actually seems that some real behaviour change takes place.

The third measure of behaviour change which was obtained was from the first section of the PIQ which was completed by the key teacher in the school with whom the team had worked. The team teacher listed up to five behaviours on which she/he had been working with the referred pupil. The school teacher then rated each of these on a five-point scale of +2 to -2, according to whether the behaviours had become much less acceptable (-2), less acceptable (-1), stayed the same (0), become more acceptable (+1), or much more acceptable (+2). The first behaviour listed was the most important to change as far as the teachers in the school were concerned. On 6 cases only one behaviour was indicated, but the majority had at least three listed. Table 3.6 shows the frequency of ratings for the first of the behaviours listed.

Table 3.6:   Frequencies of change ratings of first
             behaviour (n=223).

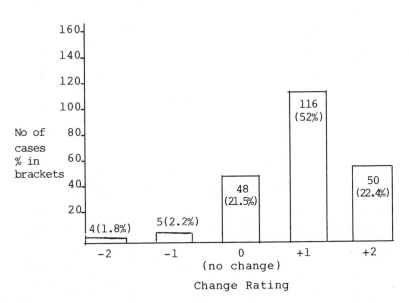

74.4% of the cases were rated as having improved
on the first (most important) behaviour originally
specified as a basis of referral. In only 9 (4%)
cases was any deterioration noted, which is all the
more remarkable since referrals often arise from a
worsening situation.

As mentioned in the earlier section, an average
behaviour change rating was computed for each case.
This was the average rating for up to five possible
behaviours that were rated. Because of the averaging,
scores are not whole numbers; therefore Table 3.7
shows that in 81.5% of cases some improvement was
noted by the teachers in schools, and that, in one
third of the cases, this improvement was rated towards the +2 end of the scale, implying considerable
improvement.

In considering these ratings, it is necessary to
be clear that they are likely to be influenced by
the school teacher's feelings about, among many
things, his/her own confidence, the pupil, and the
team teacher. The school teacher is being asked to
compare a pupil's behaviour in the present with his/
her behaviour at the time of referral. Clearly, the
memory will fade and some will exaggerate, and some
will underplay the behaviour in recalling it.

Evaluation of the work of the Support Unit

Table 3.7:   Average behaviour change ratings (n=223).

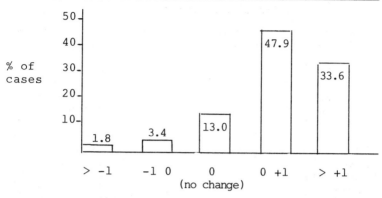

Average behaviour change rating

Possibly, over a large number of cases these distortions will cancel one another out. But, in another
sense, the distortions do not matter, since the decision a teacher makes to refer a pupil will depend
partly on some feeling that he or she requires help
in meeting the child's needs. The rating at the end
of intervention is perhaps some subjective measure
of the extent to which the teacher now feels confident to meet the child's needs, in terms of behaviour,
independently. As argued previously, disruption is a
relative concept, partly constructed by teachers'
perceptions. Having changed teachers' perceptions of
the level of disruptive activity is in many ways tantamount to changing the 'real' level of disruptive
activity. If the teachers are no longer finding a
pupil's behaviour to be unacceptable, then disruption
may be said to have ceased. Whether to ask for help
from the Support Unit will depend on a variety of
factors amongst which will be how desperate the teachers are, whether they believe intervention will
help, or whether they merely treat it as a ritual
act better done than not done. The ratings at the
end of intervention may reflect whichever of these
factors were in play. The results from the PIQ's show
that something has changed, at least in the teachers'
judgements, but also probably in the pupils' behaviour (as confirmed by the results from the BSAG's
and BC's), to make the situation more acceptable.

3.3.4 Illustrative Material: Two Case Studies, Darren and Richard.

Referral. Darren, aged 6 at the time of referral, was a member of a small infants school, and was known to teachers and helpers alike as the naughtiest boy in the school. The referral form described him as 'very naughty, refusing to work and deliberately annoying others to attract attention'. The school also mentioned that until about the age of 5, his speech had been difficult to understand and very stilted.

Assessment. The team teacher asked the class teacher to complete a Bristol Social Adjustment Guide and a Behaviour Checklist. The Guide indicated a high Ovract score (in the 2nd percentile) and concurred with the Checklist in showing Darren's high level of activity in moving round the classroom, fidgeting, and fiddling while supposed to be seated. It was also clear that he was actually not participating in many everyday conversations, e.g. greeting the teacher, talking about drawing or play, and that his main contact with other children was non-verbal, bumping into them, or pushing them. A final feature of the BSAG was the high Inconsequence score (1st percentile) which reflected Darren's apparent imperviousness to any consequences of his behaviour.

The team teacher was particularly impressed by two aspects of the referral and questionnaire data. The first was the emphasis placed on the intentionality of the behaviour, and the second was possible differences in verbal and non-verbal communication. Was the behaviour really deliberate, or was it merely so persistent and annoying that the staff were declaring their impotence by ascribing such wilful intent to the child? Was it necessary or useful to answer this question, or was it enough to acknowledge the staff's annoyance? Darren's communication pattern deserved immediate further study. A speech therapist had been involved when he was younger, and, six months previously, she had stated that he no longer had any distinct difficulties with his production of words or his use of language, and that, in time, and with the practice of everyday interaction, he would continue to progress. His hearing had also been checked recently and found normal.

The team teacher, therefore, made classroom observations, paying close attention to Darren's movements and to his pattern of communication. She noted that, over 6 half-hour sessions, he averaged 15 incidents of physical contact with another pupil when that pupil was not expecting it or inviting it, and that, when expected to be sitting down, the longest period that he remained seated was one minute, and this was while playing with lego. When the teacher was teaching them in a group (e.g. reading a story) and could, therefore, watch all of them, Darren was nearly always reprimanded when he moved or fidgeted. When the class was doing individual or small group activities, the teacher was mainly aware of Darren when other pupils complained of being pushed or bumped by him, or by a friend who appeared to copy him for fun. On these occasions, Darren was also reprimanded in front of the class. It was clear that the reprimands in whatever tone of voice had little effect on Darren's behaviour.

Formulation. The following formulation of the problem was agreed with the class teacher:
Darren's behaviour is annoying to adults and children mainly because of a high level of physical contact (15 times per half hour). He talks very little and does not sit still for long (1 minute maximum) when expected. He finds verbal communication difficult and gets little attention for it. He gets far more attention for non-verbal communication, and the physical contact with other pupils may be reinforcing in itself, in spite of the reprimands it brings. It was agreed that the objectives of intervention were
    1 to increase the level of verbal communication
and 2 to increase the length of time that Darren could sit still and be absorbed in a task.

Intervention. The class teacher thought that the first objective could not be achieved without the second. The team teacher suggested, therefore, that Darren was set tasks that were largely non-verbal, but which involved sitting down and collaboration, and that Darren would respond well to non-verbal reward as well as praise. Another problem was that Darren was associated with his friend as 'trouble' by both pupils and helpers. The class teacher suggested praising Darren for these non-verbal tasks (they were mainly construction tasks) with a 'star' pupil. The team teacher suggested making a chart - a ladder up which a snake would climb each time Darren completed a task set by the teacher, culminating in a class reward. This was put into practice.

For two weeks everything went well. It was easy to pair Darren with the 'star' pupil who was most co-operative, and the class were interested in the possibility of a reward based on Darren's progress. The team teacher was able to visit twice a week and encourage both Darren and the class teacher. After two weeks, the snake was nearing the top of

the ladder, and other pupils were complaining about
Darren less. But the class teacher was not happy.
Darren was still very fidgety in group activities
(e.g. story time). The class teacher was not prepared
to ignore Darren's fidgeting during that time, but
she did not want to exclude Darren from that time.

The team teacher agreed to observe again. It
was evident that Darren's physical contact with other
pupils had decreased (6 times per half-hour). Some
instances of other pupils touching Darren affectiona-
tely and Darren leaning back on them were noticed as
new. Also, on the construction tasks with the 'star'
pupil, it was clear that not only could Darren concentrate for 15 minutes, but also that he was very
adept at it. Perhaps it was time to think about the
first objective. If he became more confident with
verbal communication, that would increase his interest in story time, and so reduce his fidgeting and,
in turn, reduce the teacher's annoyance.

It was at this point that the class teacher ad-
mitted that she did not know how to help Darren's
language expression. This came out when the team
teacher made it clear, more as an aside than a deliberate remark, that she did not really know what progress in language development to expect from a six-
year-old. The solution was obvious. Ask the head to
ask the speech therapist to visit again. When the
team teacher visited the next week, things were still
the same. Darren was doing well on his second chart,
but the teacher was still looking less than happy.
She had not spoken to the head about the speech
therapist. In another leap of confidence in the team
teacher, the class teacher said that she found it
hard to talk to the head. Darren's was not the only
problem of communication. The team teacher agreed
that sometimes she had found the head difficult to
talk to, and they decided that the team teacher would
ask the head into Darren's class to see the progress
of the chart. The head was pleased. The following day,
the class teacher asked the head about the speech
therapist. Fortunately, the speech therapist was able
to come in the following week, when the class teacher
made it clear that all she wanted was some discussion
about what language development to expect from Darren
and some suggestions for materials to use with him.
The speech therapist suggested some group language
games. The class teacher tried these and, although
progress was slow, his attention to the spoken word
and his self-confidence grew. Within four weeks, the
class teacher was able to report that, although he
was still fidgety during story time, he did listen

better, and she felt less annoyed with him and largely ignored him.

Evaluation. After two terms the case was closed, because the class teacher and head teacher felt that
they did not need further help from the team teacher.
A 2nd British Social Adjustment Guide showed a score
at the 20th percentile on Ovract, and a 2nd Checklist showed a dramatic reduction in the number and
frequency of behaviour relating to physical contact
against other pupils, although fidgeting and fiddling were still a bit of a problem.

The baldness of these statistics hides the fluctuations in progress that the history of the intervention shows. The pattern of change is not an un-
common one. Some change in behaviour management leads
to quite a rapid behaviour change on the pupil's
part. In this case. the change was perhaps accelera-
ted by the ready co-operation and adaptability of
other pupils. The sticking point came when the class
teacher had to change her behaviour quite radically
- either she had to do something about story time,
which seemed very important to her, or else she had
to admit her reluctance about language teaching.

Richard.

Referral. Richard was 13 years old at the time of
referral, and attending a mixed comprehensive school.
Staff were concerned about Richard's difficult behaviour both in and outside the classroom - he did
very little work including homework, he was rude towards staff and was generally uncooperative both
with staff and with pupils. Outside the classroom,
he was often involved in fights, and difficulties
arose in class as a result of them.

Assessment. The Bristol Social Adjustment Guides
completed by two teachers, showed that Richard was
perceived to be extremely over-reactive (3rd percentile), and that the main component of this was hostility towards both adults and peers. Also, one teacher
observed that some of his behaviour was rather withdrawn and lethargic, giving a not insignificant
score on the under-reactive scale. The Behaviour
Checklist confirmed the antagonistic nature of the
problem behaviour, and at least showed that his behaviour was acceptable as far as noise and movement
in the class were concerned. Teachers also mentioned
that Richard was asthmatic and, on two occasions,
his fights had resulted in severe attacks of asthma.
Richard was observed in 12 different lessons. It was
clear that he did not do much work (on task 50% of
the time, although that was more than some teachers
had expected). Very little rudeness and no fights

were observed in the classroom, although teachers felt that the presence of an observer might have inhibited this. This, in itself, was interesting because it did indicate that Richard had some degree of self-control. Three playground fights were reported during a two-week assessment period. In the classrooms, the team teacher noticed a greater degree of minor irritating behaviour than expected from Richard - in terms of ignoring the teacher, muttering, turning away, asking for things at inconvenient moments - which clearly affected the teachers, though they were not always aware of how much. What sometimes happened was that Richard was blamed for something which he had not done. This increased Richard's resentment. On looking at Richard's standard of work, it was also clear that he had more than a little difficulty with reading and writing. Although he was receiving some help from a 'remedial' teacher, some other teachers did not seem to be making allowances for his difficulties.

Formulation. The team teacher arrived at a very simple formulation to which two teachers in the school also contributed. Richard was receiving a lot of teacher attention for his unacceptable behaviour and not enough encouragement for more acceptable ways of behaving, or for his efforts at work. This only served to build up resentment in a boy who, in any case, was inclined to feel hard done by because of his asthma.

The objectives of intervention were:

1 to develop and extend the acceptable behaviour which Richard already showed

2 to sensitise teachers to his work difficulties.

Intervention. As a first step towards this, the team teacher decided to see Richard on his own a few times. Having built up some trust, the team teacher put it to Richard that, although he may be unfairly blamed sometimes, there were aspects of his classroom behaviour that created difficulties. Richard and the team teacher looked at the problem as one of self-control, and as a first step, they decided to try and monitor what Richard thought that he could already control. They designed and made a monitoring-booklet to ask teachers for comment on three areas each lesson: preparing to start a task, getting the teacher's attention, and listening. A meeting of all Richard's subject teachers was held, and they agreed to complete the booklet for three weeks, and to encourage Richard as much as possible. The head of year agreed to look at the booklet with Richard each day; the team teacher saw him weekly, as well as going into some classes. The consistency with which the staff kept up their entries in the booklet was remarkable, and all went well. The scheme was extended for another three weeks. Staff were more concerned now that Richard was not getting work completed and that there were still fights in the playground. However, the general attitude towards him was more positive and sympathetic.

It was Richard himself who brought the problem of his work to the team teacher, who started to role-play with him ways of asking teachers for help. They substituted this for getting the teacher's attention in the monitoring booklet. Richard and the teachers kept the booklets up for a term, but moving to a weekly rather than a daily basis. By the end, the teachers were more sensitive to Richard's difficulties, and some were asking the 'remedial' teachers for suggestions about how to help him more. Playground fights were still a problem, but teachers were more inclined to pay attention to Richard's side of the story. Eventually, they decided together with the team teacher to tackle the problem as one for the group as a whole. This was done by the form tutor and the team teacher during tutor group time.

Evaluation. The intervention was evaluated after two terms by a second BSAG and a second Behaviour Checklist. The Ovract score had reduced to the 18th percentile, and also the Unract score had reduced to the 40th percentile. The classroom behaviour on the Checklist showed very few problems, except some hostility towards other pupils. Teachers also spontaneously wrote comments that they had noticed some improvement in Richard's writing and amount of work completed. Clearly, work was still to be done on his attainments and on his relationships with other pupils. It was remarkable how quickly the hostility broke down both on the teachers' and on Richard's part, when in the past report books, talks with the head of year, and letters home had had no effect. Staff commented later that they had particularly valued seeing the team teacher in so many classes as an observer. This was in spite of the fact that, at first, the school had been very suspicious of classroom observation, and most teachers taught behind closed doors. After the hostility had broken down, the path of progress on Richard's attainments was much slower and required the persistence of both the teachers and Richard.

Evaluation of the work of the Support Unit

3.4 The performance of other children in the class.

3.4.1 Methods of data collection.
This seemed a crucial variable to try to assess, since much of the argument for segregating pupils whose behaviour is perceived as disruptive does not centre on the therapeutic benefit for those pupils, but on the notion of the improved performance of the rest of the class in the calm atmosphere which would exist in the absence of such pupils. However, it was necessary to be mindful of the amount of work which would be entailed for teachers in supplying data. Furthermore, if measures of attainment and behaviour were simply taken at the beginning and end of the team's involvement, any changes could hardly be attributed to the intervention of the team on disruptive behaviour. To make such inferences with any degree of confidence would necessitate an elaborate, experimental model with control groups to allow for other inputs apart from the team's intervention. The most straightforward and economical method seemed to be to include a section in the Post-Intervention Questionnaire for teacher in schools to complete.

This section simply asked for a rating on a five-point scale of the effects of intervention on the rest of the class, in terms of a) their educational achievement, and b) their behaviour. On this scale a rating of +2 indicates 'much better', +1 'better', 0 'the same', -1 'worse' and -2 'much worse'. It would be quite possible for teachers to rate the effect of intervention on the educational levels of the rest of the class as making things worse, if the interventions were such that the teachers had to devote so much time to the referred pupil(s) that the rest of the class were neglected. On the other hand, following the rotten apple analogy, it is possible that the rest of the class is contaminated, as it were, by the behaviour of one or two pupils. In such a case, improvements in the behaviour of these pupils could lead to improvements for the whole class. But we were interested in the education and behaviour of the rest of the class for more practical measures than examining the hopes and fears of parents and teachers based on reference to barrels of apples.

According to the social learning perspective espoused by the team, the attainment and behaviour of the rest of the class would be crucial in helping to maintain the behaviour (acceptable or otherwise) of the referred pupil. Indeed, peer pressure and response might have played a part in generating the

behaviour in the first place. The rotten apple analogy is, then, deceptive since the interaction between
a pupil and the rest of the class is not one-way, but
two-way. Indeed, social learning theory would only
see a pupil's behaviour as comprehensible within the
context of the rest of the class. Following this
argument, the team's interventions were often as much
with the context as with the referred pupil. Interventions can involve teachers and, indeed, a pupil's
peer group. For these reasons, interventions might
be expected to have effects on the rest of the class
as well as on the referred pupil.

3.4.2 Results.

Tables 3.8 and 3.9 show that the teachers felt
that the intervention had a positive effect on the
behaviour and attainment of the rest of the class.
The importance of this perception cannot be over-
emphasised, as it means that the policy of keeping
a referred pupil in class rather than segregating
him or her, far from holding back or contaminating
the rest of the class actually benefits them, as a
spin-off from Support Unit intervention. The effect
on the behaviour of the rest of the class might have
been readily predicted, since this may be directly
influenced by much of the Support Unit's work with
teachers in school.

Table 3.8:   The effect of intervention on the rest
             of the class' attainment.

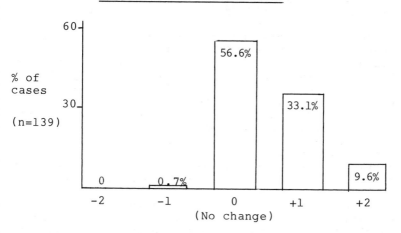

Table 3.9: <u>The effect of intervention on the rest of the class' behaviour.</u>

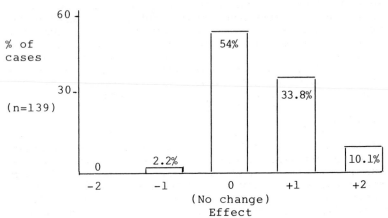

The effect on attainment is more surprising, yet of such significance that it perhaps warrants a larger research project with control groups in order to test this finding as stringently as possible. The implication is that teacher effectiveness can be enhanced by support which is:-
1. specific and problem-solving rather than general advisory;
2. practical and based on a shared classroom experience;
3. non-specialist (team teachers do not claim expertise in any particular curriculum areas);
4. regular and probably at least weekly;
5. systematic in its approach.

3.5 <u>The skills and confidence of individual teachers in schools to manage disruptive behaviour.</u>

3.5.1 <u>Methods of data collection.</u>
This aspect of the team's work has always seemed important, since the support provided is as much to teachers as to pupils. But any support is counter-productive if it becomes a crutch which cannot be thrown away. Good support is enabling. If it were possible to increase the skills and confidence of the school teachers, with whom the team worked, with regard to disruptive behaviour, then this might influence a whole generation of pupils with whom this teacher might go on to work. The long-term spin-offs here are considerable indeed. This variable is not, however, an easy one to assess. Such assess-

ment could lead to mistrust in a work context
which depends on trust. The evaluation was limited,
therefore, to asking teachers with whom the team had
worked to assess themselves, on a case by case basis,
on the extent to which their confidence had increased
or decreased as a result of working with a team teacher. A section of the Post-Intervention Questionnaire asked "If similar behaviours.occurred in the
future, would you feel more or less confident of
being able to handle them?" The questionnaire provided a rating scale of -2 to +2.

3.5.2 Results.
Table 3.10 shows that, on the PIQ's over 57%
of teachers stated that they would be more confident
in handling similar disruptive behaviour in the future. This is perhaps surprising, in that with team
teachers, supposedly having been appointed for their
expertise with disruptive behaviour, coming into
their classrooms, the teachers in schools might be
expected to feel de-skilled.

Table 3.10:   Changes in the confidence of teachers
               in handling similar disruptive behaviour
               in the future.

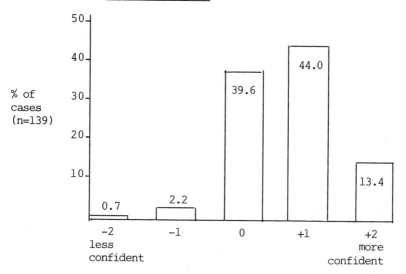

One of the aims of the team has always been to
share skills both within itself and with teachers
in schools. However, unless in-service training is
explicitly requested by a teacher or group of

teachers, or unless it is agreed following a formulation, then it is usually an aim implicit in working in schools rather than one which is overtly stated. So, if teachers in schools actually feel more confident as a result of intervention, this is an important vindication of the method of support evolved by the team. The spread of results in Table 3.10 indicates that the results have some validity, despite the limitations of being based on teachers' self-assessment: some were not inhibited from reporting a loss in confidence and a sizeable proportion (nearly 40%) reported no change. The validity of the results was further enhanced when data from the PIQ were cross-tabulated: one finding was that the greater the behaviour change reported for the pupil, the greater was the likelihood of the teacher's reporting increased confidence.

3.6 The way schools as organisations conceptualise and deal with problems of behaviour.

3.6.1 Methods of data collection.
There were many aspects of school organisation and policy which could have been incorporated in a data collection before the team ever began its work. Pressure to begin casework, as well as ambivalence towards the putative policy of the Support Unit on the part of schools, made any systematic data collection of these variables impossible. Nevertheless, the team were interested in how schools explained the causes of disruption, the relative emphases placed on the urban environment, parents, peer group, curriculum, personality, classroom organisation, school rules, and teaching style. The team also examined the different ways the schools organised themselves to help reduce disruption, since it was possible that effective ideas and good practice could be passed between schools. Some schools provided information on these matters in their school booklets. Most secondary schools had a system whereby a pupil was sent to a series of teachers, usually head of department, year, or house, and then on to a deputy or the head teacher for serious incidents which might warrant exclusion or suspension. Schools differed according to who was informed about disruptive behaviour: some insisting that the head teacher was told about every incident where parents were informed, others leaving it to the discretion of the head of house or year. In primary schools, the arrangements for dealing with disruptive behaviour were more likely to be centred on the head.

Some primary and secondary schools had well defined criteria for what disciplinary action should be taken for what behaviour; other schools operated on a more informal basis.

At least one school saw the formulation of the Support Unit as a response to the abolition of corporal punishment, and many were working out alternative strategies to caning. Various systems of report books, detentions, house marks, letters home, interviews with pupils and/or parents, and time-out rooms were being evolved. Most of the information about these aspects of school organisation, however, was gathered informally, and was far from systematic. A flavour of the extreme attitudes of some staff can be discerned from the illustrative material (3.6.3) below.

Limited in terms of systematic data collection on this aspect of the team's work, initial concentration was confined to examining time spent by different members of staff on disruptive behaviour. A distinction was made between class or subject teachers and senior teachers (heads of house/year/ department, deputies and head teachers). In one section of the PIQ teachers were asked to rate an increase or decrease in time spent by the class teachers and senior teachers on each pupil with whom the team worked, both during the period of intervention and after it. The ratings were on a scale of -2 to +2.

After three years of the team's operation, it was felt appropriate to look in more detail at how schools dealt with disruptive behaviour. Interviews, rather than questionnaires, were chosen as yielding richer information, despite the fact that the time commitment involved meant that only a sample of cases could be taken. One of the authors took twenty random cases from those referred after September 1982, and independently approached the school teachers with whom the team worked on these cases. A structured interview schedule was devised, after some piloting, so that answers could be compared across interviews. In this way a picture was built up of how a school had organised itself to handle behaviour problems, and of how the work of a team teacher had interposed itself into that organisation. One feature of the interviews was that three perspectives on the same situation were sought. For each of the twenty cases, the pupil, the team teacher and a key teacher in the school were interviewed. It was not possible, however, for most of the pupils to comment in much detail on the school organisation.

Evaluation of the work of the Support Unit

Most of the information on this issue came, therefore, from the interviews with teachers (the same
questions were asked of the team teacher and the
school teacher). The two perspectives, one from within and one from without, provided interesting com-
parisons.

3.6.2 Results.

Table 3.11 Changes in time spent by school staff
during and after intervention with
referred pupils.

	-2		-1		0		+1		+2	
	During	After	During	After	During	After	During	After	During	After
*	10.6	21.9	16.3	19.3	53.7	46.5	14.6	9.6	4.9	2.6
#	11.7	19.0	16.4	25.6	48.4	33.9	17.2	18.2	6.3	3.3

Changes in time spent

*Senior staff
#Class or subject teacher

Figures are % 137 cases

Table 3.11 is capable of more than one interpretation. The key question is whether the time spent
by staff on the referred pupil was positive or negative. Even if there was no change in time spent during the course of or after intervention, there
might have been a change in the quality of the contact - from negative to positive, or vice versa. The
information obtained from the PIQ does not allow
assumptions about the quality of the contact to be
made, though information on this is available from
the results of the interviews.
    Table 3.11 does show that in a significant pro-
portion of cases, both senior staff and class or
subject teachers rated themselves as spending less
time with a referred pupil after intervention than
during it. On the assumption that this does not mean
that the teacher is actually spending less time with
that pupil than, proportionately, with others (which
is fairly unlikely), then the reduction in time
spent is probably desirable. Disruptive behaviour is
often time-consuming, and it often directs teachers'

time and attention disproportionately to a few pupils, particularly boys. It is, then, desirable to reduce the time spent by staff on referred pupils closer to levels appropriate to other pupils in the class or school. The amount of time spent with other pupils would then seem not to be suffering, and their education not to be disrupted by the behaviour of the referred pupil.

The interviews conducted in 1983 gave more detailed insight into the part that support team intervention played in the way schools conceptualise and deal with disruptive behaviour. One interview question asked the teacher to state what behaviour the pupil under discussion exhibited that was considered a problem. A subsequent question asked the teacher to generate hypotheses about how pupils who behaved in such a way were different from those who did not. The responses to this question were analysed and placed into categories. Where a teacher offered more than one response, each was given equal weighting in assigning them to categories. Thus, the categories in Table 3.12 were derived from responses to open questions and were not suggested to the teachers.

Table 3.12 shows that there are differences between how school teachers and team teachers conceptualise behaviour problems. The categories are not quite mutually exclusive, and conceal many shades of meaning. However, they point to differences in the ways in which the two groups of teachers examine a problem, look for intervention, and determine who is responsible. Thus, the team teachers tended to look first for within-child factors: learning ability, social learning, behavioural characteristics (such as paying little attention to consequences or restlessness). Since all of these may be improved by providing a learning environment appropriate to the pupil's needs, the responsibility for change rests clearly with the teacher and the pupil. The school teachers, on the other hand, tended to look first at home factors. Lack of parental care, changes of address, "unstable home life", "upsetting childhood" were all ideas which were put forward. The responsibility for change, here, is shifted away from the school and the teachers. In the course of collaboration, school teachers and support teachers must negotiate their different accounts of disruptive behaviour.

Table 3.12:   School teachers' and team teachers'
               ideas about the 'causes' of behaviour
               problems (% responses).

	Home circumstances	Within child	Peer group influence	Other
(n=20) School teachers	60	30	5	5
(n=20) Team teachers	12	72	11	5

In studying the twenty cases in detail, it became clear that the role of the team teacher varied considerably from case to case. In terms of contacts and communications the team teacher could be involved with any combination of up to five or more participants: pupil, teacher, senior teacher (head), pastoral teacher (tutor in a secondary school) and parent(s). Detailed account of two of the cases illustrate these varying patterns of communication.

The first case is that of a boy in junior school who refuses to conform to class rules and, if he wants attention from the teacher, simply shouts out. The class teacher is exasperated. She keeps the head teacher informed about the boy. The head informs the mother about him and she, in turn, gets angry and exasperated with her son. At the outset of referral, the communication could be represented thus:-

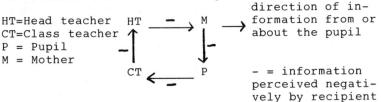

HT=Head teacher
CT=Class teacher
P = Pupil
M = Mother

direction of information from or about the pupil

- = information perceived negatively by recipient

The team teacher starts by receiving all the information about the pupil from the teachers, and also makes contact with the pupil and his mother. The team teacher begins to perceive the boy positively and feeds that back carefully to class teacher and mother. The team teacher negotiates a supportive role towards both class teacher and mother and keeps the head teacher informed.

Evaluation of the work of the Support Unit

The communication flow then looks like this:-

TT = Team teacher
+ = information
    perceived
    positively by
    recipient

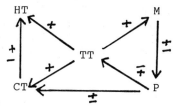

The perception of the boy by the class teacher and the mother begin to change as a consequence of the positive feedback. They start to manage his difficult behaviour more calmly and to focus more on ways of encouraging some other aspects of his behaviour. The head teacher, too, is kept informed and no longer feels the pressure from the boy through the class teacher, which was previously passed on to the mother.

The second case is that of a boy in the third year of secondary school, noisy, rude to teachers, not making friends. On gathering the information, the team teacher realised that the boy's form tutor had spent a lot of time getting to know the boy, and saw him in a somewhat different light from the head of year, who had made the referral. The pattern at the outset of referral was like this:-

FT = Form Tutor
HoY = Head of Year
STs = Subject Teachers

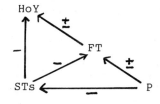

It was the head of year who had made the referral, but it was the form tutor who was having to hold the conflicting information. The form tutor was in fact in an analogous position to that in which team teachers sometimes find themelves. However, the form tutor had no clear means of resolving the institutional conflict, being an insider in the school. The team teacher took on positive perceptions of the boy from the boy, negative perceptions of him from the head of year, and mixed perceptions from the form tutor. The team teacher held joint discussions with the head of year and form tutor. This had the effect of encouraging more positive perceptions, enabling them to share ideas more evenly, and establishing a

pattern of regular support for the form tutor from
the head of year. With the attention of the form
tutor and the team teacher, the boy's behaviour began to improve. This helped the head of year who was
beginning to speak with more conviction to subject
teachers about the boy's more positive side. The
communication pattern during intervention was:-

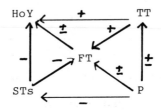

These two cases illustrate a process that appeared to be general amongst all the twenty cases
studied. This process seems to follow certain principles, if communication within school organisations
is to be facilitated:-
1. the team teacher focuses on the behaviour, not
   the child as a person;
2. the team teacher focuses on positive aspects of
   the child's behaviour as well as negative;
3. the team teacher does not replace any existing
   structures of support for the pupil or the teachers or the parents, but attempts to energise
   them or run in parallel with them;
4. the team teacher does not leave out of an information chain any person who was previously in one;
5. the team teacher accepts that perceptions of a
   pupil's behaviour are not necessarily in step with
   the pupil's actual behaviour.

3.6.3 Illustrative material : a personal and retro-spective account of a staff meeting.

The most dramatic, if not the most memorable meeting
I ever had, as teacher-in-charge, with a staff group
was at an evening staff meeting in a large secondary
school. This was right at the beginning of the scheme
when I was going round the division, giving talks at
staff meetings, trying to ensure that everybody knew
what we were hoping to achieve. Looking back I think
it was rather more than a huge public relations
exercise. Certainly, it allowed me to explain to
large numbers of mainstream teachers how the Support
Unit was going to work, to stress its advantages,
clarify its limitations, and to guide appropriate
referrals. But it also gave me a chance to listen to

Evaluation of the work of the Support Unit

the kinds of expectations teachers had of the team,
and to try to initiate ways of working with a specific school. For this reason, and so as not to un-
dermine the team teacher's credibility, I always
went to such meetings along with the team member who
was responsible for the school in question.

There were, at this stage, several vociferously
expressed reservations about the ability of any team
of people to do the job for which the Support Unit
was established. We were aware of sharp criticism
if not hostility. One of the team had had printed for
me a tee-shirt with the caption Support Your Support
Team. That was rather the way we were feeling -
though I never actually wore the tee-shirt to a staff
meeting.

For myself I suppose it was meetings such as
these which gave me credibility and authority with
the rest of the team. They were able to see me not
only lending tangible assistance, but also dealing
reasonably competently with large, often difficult,
groups. When these meetings were successful, they
usually increased the status as well as the visibi-
lity of the team member within a particular school.

The staff of this secondary school were known
to be hostile to the scheme, the head, the deputies,
and apparently the entire staff. They had wanted an
off-site sin bin, and were appalled at the idea that
a bunch of young teachers were going to swan in and
tell them how to deal with difficult kids. It was
this impression that I was intent on correcting, as
well as perhaps getting a chance to stress some of
the advantages, as I saw it, for pupils to be able
to remain in the mainstream.

The team teacher and I, a little nervous in our
Sunday best, were received by the head and the deputies. Perhaps the person-to-person contact persuaded them that polite disagreement would be preferable
to the confrontation I had been anticipating. There
were even a few smiles and pleasantries over the cups
of tea before we were led into the staff room.

The layout here was very formal with the head,
myself and the team teacher seated behind tables,
facing the massed rows of members of staff. There
was, however, a slight oddity in the arrangement in
that, perhaps because of the large numbers, a partition had been opened into an adjoining room, and many
of the staff were seated in here, largely out of
sight of those positioned behind the tables. As the
head was rapidly getting through the school business
which preceded our slot in the meeting, the odd
whispered conversation could be heard from this part

of the gathering, the crackling of newspaper, even the occasional giggle. The members of the Jockey Club, one felt, were preparing for another piece of, doubtless obscene, pretentious silliness from that beast Stravinsky.

I stood up and briefly described the work of the Unit. Don't tell them everything, I reminded myself, leave them some things to elicit by questions, and keep yourself material for substantial answers. I stressed modesty: "We are not imagining that we have more skills with classroom disruption than other people in the school. How could we? We simply were working from our humble experience, but did have the free time and the organisation to do those things to improve disrupted situations that doubtless pastoral staff, and indeed all teachers in the school, would do, were they fortunate enough to have the space". Reminding myself to be careful not to lay it on with a trowel, I stressed that we wanted to listen to their ideas, that we did not have any hard and fast plan that we hoped to impose on the school. This was certainly correct: we wanted to evolve with them a successful way of working. Perhaps it was at this point that I used the phrase "we could discuss it in a context less gladiatorial than this" or perhaps it was in answer to a question. But I am certain that it was with this phrase that I won the sympathy and agreement of the head which I was never to lose. Whether it was an enhanced perception of the lonely beleaguered figure I cut, or whether the image itself appealed to the imagination of an old classicist, I do not know, but at least one member of my audience suddenly had his thumb pointing towards the ceiling. The rustling of newspapers continued from behind the partition, however, accompanied by the occasional half-heard remark and repressed laughter.

Nevertheless, listening to the questions I was aware that my little talk had evoked criticisms that were not directed at me, but through me towards the school organisation itself. "Wasn't it true that the only way to deal with these kids was to stop being lenient and continue with forceful corporal punishment?"

"On the contrary, could not you as an expert on these matters, confirm that corporal punishment was not only morally degrading, but totally ineffective?"

"Have I been mistaken, or is not a large part of the job you are describing the work of those members of the pastoral staff who have been rewarded with scale fours for fulfilling such duties?"

Evaluation of the work of the Support Unit

"Who would the Support Unit work with, the classroom teachers who were at the forefront of the battle, or only with heads and deputies?"

Perhaps it is only in retrospect that I see the partitioned staff room as an image of the division among the staff body. But, at the time, I was aware that the notoriously high level of disruption in this school needed to be understood partly in terms of the conflict between members of the teaching staff. This conflict appeared to be not just a "them and us" disagreement with the head and deputies, but a more general cynicism in which no teacher was prepared to give any credibility to anything said by a colleague outside his/her tiny circle or clique.

This was a school from which the Unit subsequently received many referrals. A way of working was eventually evolved which proved to satisfy at least some sections of the staff. Interestingly, the team teacher initially worked very closely with the head and deputies, trying to clarify what teachers in the school wanted not of the Unit, but of their management and pastoral personnel. This eventually led to intense work with the pastoral staff, rationalising their routines and facilitating contact both within the school and with other outside agencies.

As far as I myself was concerned, it was encounters such as these which made clear to me the boundaries of the possible. I remained convinced that behaviour could not be changed without concentrating on the environment and the context as well as on the referred child. But I was made forcefully aware of how difficult it is for large, complex organisations to change, especially when the agents of change are relatively low status peripatetic teachers.

Chapter 4

CLASSROOM PRACTICE

4.1 Intervening in classrooms.

This chapter will focus on the work of support
teachers in classrooms and consider the implications
for class teachers and support teachers, if we accept
the implications of the previous chapter that this
sort of work helps to prevent classroom disruption.
In chapter 2, the term 'intervention'was introduced,
and the various forms that this could take in the
classroom were enumerated. Chapter 3 considered the
effects of such intervention on pupils, teachers and
schools, and suggested that the methods of the support team were vindicated by the positive outcomes.
This chapter looks in detail at the practicalities
of intervening in classrooms. After an introductory
section on the professional issues of classroom intervention, we will go on to describe work with teachers exclusively, work with teachers and individual
pupils simultaneously, work with individual pupils,
then work with individual pupils and their parents,
and finally work with groups of pupils.
    We start by examining professional issues of how
a teacher intervenes in another teacher's classroom
practice. There is an image of autonomy often connected with the professionalism of teachers whereby,
once the door of the classroom is closed, what goes
on inside it is the teacher's business and no-one
else's. This often extends to the curriculum. Teachers
in a school may meet in departmental groups to discuss their curriculum plans, guidelines may be issued
by the LEA or by the DES, advisers may be asked into
or sent into the school for specific curriculum areas,
but these sources of outside input may do no more
than make superficial changes in the actual substance
of lessons. With regard to disruptive behaviour, this
automony may become an embarrassingly serious issue.

If teachers in a school know that one or two of their colleagues are having difficulties with classroom behaviour, then they may not necessarily mention it to the teachers themselves, nor bring it to the attention of those in authority. On the one hand, this might be seen as interfering with the professional autonomy of a colleague, on the other as causing him or her difficulties with the head teacher.

A further consideration is involved here in that, for many teachers, the admission of difficulties with classroom control is perceived to be a form of failure. Even those most committed to the teaching profession seem to find it hard to discuss their part in classroom difficulties with colleagues on the staff. They will discuss what they perceive to be personality attributes of individual children, or the merits or otherwise of curriculum material. But to mention their own teaching behaviour is somehow to break a conspiracy of silence. This is clearly an exaggerated picture of what is nevertheless an extensive practice, which any amount of management courses, school conferences, creation of special posts in schools, has not succeeded in overcoming. There is, indeed, a danger that those most in need of tangible assistance with classroom disruption will be the ones least likely to receive it, because to mention that such help were needed would be to come out from behind the shield of teacherly professional autonomy.

Given this, there are obvious obstacles to the work of the support team teachers. Since these teachers themselves are on Scale 3 and, in some cases comparatively young, they are within a familiar hierarchical pattern and yet, being outside the structure of the school, they do not fit. A youngish teacher from outside the school, who claims some expertise on such a highly sensitive issue as disruption, may well be perceived as a threat. What the team teacher needs to do is to offer help without implying criticism, to share professional notions of autonomy rather than to offer a defence, to encourage clear accounts of events without seeming to pry or to be likely to report back harmfully to senior colleagues. This seems like a fairly tall order. Whatever the state of personal relationships between a team teacher and teachers in schools, this knife edge between trust and mistrust remains in the background. It may, on the other hand, be what keeps the relationship alive and working, whereas staff within schools quickly discover how far their own personal relationships can go and settle into established patterns.

The question of how team teachers present themselves in schools and how they maintain positive and productive contact with all sorts of staff is as much a matter for team policy as it is for individual members. Indeed, in our case, we saw from the outset that getting to a position to be able to do the job was actually an important part of it. Indeed, many of the skills of tact and diplomacy necessary to get to that position were closely related to those likely to result in the job being performed with any success. The policies which the team adopted concerned staff selection and training, the public relations of the team as a whole, an adherence to an overt professionalism and specifically formulated procedures.

To take each of these briefly in turn, staff selection and training is vital. Team teachers need to have both professional experience and personal qualities that gain credibility with teachers. The critical professional background would appear to be some solid experience of mainstream schools as well as of some aspects of special education. Some qualification or confirmed interest in educational psychology or the sociology of education is also advantageous. Further, no-one would be likely to be appointed who did not have a clear and enthusiastic commitment to the work of the team, and who did not accept the significance of the training and supervision procedures outlined in Chapter 2. These qualities would be in addition to the sine qua non that they would be able to manage most disruptive behaviour in a positive and successful way. These criteria seem hard enough to meet, but gaps can partly be filled by training. What is more difficult to select for and train for are those more indefinable attributes that so many interviewers seek. It is essential to send into schools people who can present themselves with both confidence and modesty, without appearing threatening or threatened, people who can deal with emotional, embarrassing or challenging situations with other adults, and respond with calmness, positive suggestions and humour. What is sought and what is encouraged through role-play and simulations in in-service training is personal style and presentation which gives team teachers at least some skills and confidence in overcoming uneasiness or defensiveness when they encounter teachers in schools.

The profile of the Support Team in schools was always fairly high. This was adopted as a deliberate but high-risk policy in the face of not a few schools who would have preferred the conventional sin bin to a peripatetic team. The risk was that the team would not live up to its publicity. If such a team were established with less controversy, then it may not be necessary to adopt a high profile. Whatever the case, the aim is to provide some credibility for team teachers. As isolated teachers working in a variety of schools, often with people of higher status than themselves, they need to show support and a certain measure of authority from the public image of the team as a whole. Of course, the maintenance of this image and credibility must be based on real achievement and is the responsibility of all members of the team. However, it is possible for certain members of the team, particularly the teacher in charge, to cultivate a high profile as a matter of policy. This can be done by giving staff meetings in schools to explain the team's work and to attempt to answer any questions on difficulties (see the illustrative material at the end of chapter 3). This can be a productive way of facilitating a team teacher's work in a school by clarifying the role and by deflecting any criticism. It is a practice that needs to be repeated periodically in order to review objectives in a given school, and to re-negotiate roles if necessary. Another way of developing the team's profile is to run courses in schools or teachers' centres, by contributing to the induction of probationary teachers, and by playing a significant role in local educational policy discussions.

The encouragement of professionalism among team teachers is in some ways an attempt to meet those difficulties in intervention concerned with teacher autonomy in their own terms. Professionalism can often mean simply what one approves of, so it is as well to be specific. In addition to aspects of demeanour and social skills, touched on earlier, confidentiality is an important element of the team teacher's professionalism. This does, of course, apply equally to relationships with pupils and parents, but it is crucial when working with teachers. Teachers and heads need to be assured of two forms of confidentiality: firstly, that team teachers can be given some information in absolute confidence, and secondly that information that is passed on, especially outside the school, will be for professional purposes only, and will not be debased into gossip or negative talk about their difficulties either with other members of staff or in other schools. Thus, it is good practice for team teachers to discuss cases amongst themselves without giving names of pupils, schools, or teachers. This is part of the process of treating colleagues in school with respect. This respect acknowledges and even expects a commensurate professionalism on their part. Thus, the class teacher's autonomy mentioned above is always respected: a team teacher would never enter a classroom either for observation or intervention without first having obtained the consent of the class teacher.

Another way of demonstrating professionalism and of eliciting the same is to talk in strictly educational terms, to see difficulties as not to do with personalities, or success and failure, but rather with educational variables - curriculum, grouping, seating, pupils' skills - which teachers are admirably suited to discuss and resolve. Clearly, in time, formality does relax and personal relationships do develop. But they are always best maintained if simple signs of professionalism remain - punctuality, responding to letters and phone calls promptly, brief and accurate record keeping.

The procedures which the Support Team adopted, described in Chapter 2, were designed to be of assistance in casework. They have the further advantage, however, of helping to provide rituals for formalising interventions in schools. Teachers must ask for assistance by completing a referral form or suggesting to a colleague that one is completed before any intervention is possible. The referral form always asks for the name of a teacher recommending the referral, as well as the signature of a senior member of staff. This gives the team teacher two points of contact in the school, one at a teacher level, the other at an administrative level. There are further stages of questionnaire completion and discussion, providing opportunities for starchy politeness, relaxation, or resistance, before potentially more threatening matters arise. The process of joint formulation of the problem between team teachers and school teachers is particularly helpful in this respect. The bureaucratic task of jointly completing a form to summarise the assessment provides a structure for discussion and concentrates minds on areas of agreement and positive action. Evaluation and review procedures likewise provide a formal and pre-planned opportunity where, if necessary, disagreements and disappointments can be brought to light and alternative responses considered.

It is important to stress the innovative nature of this work. Certainly, other groups of professionals, such as educational psychologists, regularly work as teams intervening in schools. But they have certain status advantages (no matter how this is seen) over a group of Scale 3 teachers, and they have an area of expertise and professional procedure on which to rely which is substantially different from the skills of the teachers with whom they are working. The Support Team teacher, by contrast, may be regarded as just another teacher with little to offer beyond the expertise which already exists in the school. Indeed, this is an image which the support teachers are likely to encourage. If their expertise is seen as being educational and what they have to offer consists of a bit of time, a certain degree of experience and access to back-up services, then they can hope to assist in the business of teaching in schools. Furthermore, if their skills are regarded as part of good educational practice, and not a matter of mystique or esoteric knowledge, then there is every hope that teachers in schools will see these skills as something they can legitimately and without too much difficulty develop themselves. A further difference between the work of the team teachers and that of educational psychologists is that the latter can often focus their attention firmly on the referred pupil. They are then not seen as a threat to teachers. On the contrary, the model of individual casework and the high possibility of referral to segregated special provision is likely to confirm teachers' views that the difficulties are centred in the child (and perhaps in his/her home) and are not something to do with the functioning of specific teachers or the school as an institution. By contrast, the aim of the team teachers is to discourage the process of attributing all the difficulties to the child, and to try to develop in schools and teachers the skills and flexibility to advocate the referred child successfully without recourse to a segregated placement. In many ways the team teachers, far from relieving the school of difficulties, are likely to turn them back upon the class teachers and the head teacher - although with some tangible assistance.

In stressing these excitingly innovative features of the support teachers' work, there is a risk of describing it as a series of con-tricks. The above paragraphs could be read as depictions of methods of encouraging servility, fawning and devious manipulation among the team teachers, as if the main component of the team's in-service training was learning how to chat up school personnel. In fact, this is not the case. In order to work effectively in schools, it is necessary to establish positive relations with the people who work there. If this is not done, there are risks of not receiving further referrals, of having proposals vetoed and casework made almost impossible, of becoming a figure of suspicion or contempt in the staffroom. Working as an outsider in schools is never easy, and haphazard attitudes to the regularity, etiquette and formalities of visiting are unlikely ever to develop the credibility needed to perform effective work with teachers and children. It is the nature of this work on classroom disruption that we now go on to describe.

4.2 Work with teachers.

It is possible to intervene on the case of a referred child and to diminish appreciably his or her participation in classroom disruption without ever having face to face contact with the pupil. Indeed, the pupil need never know that anyone other than his normal teacher(s) have been working with him or her. The focus of intervention is not the pupil but the teacher(s). The aim is to develop skills, confidence and flexibility whereby the teacher continues to educate the pupil without any more tangible assistance than discussion and advice. There are three major advantages to this method of working. Firstly, with regard to the referred pupil, it causes the very minimum of disturbance to the pattern of his or her education. He or she is not singled out and stigmatised, nor made to feel special either in his or her own eyes or in those of peers. The opportunities to develop a deviant reputation with family, school staff or other pupils are severely diminished. Secondly, if a teacher or group of teachers can develop the skills and confidence successfully to educate a referred pupil, then there is a high likelihood that these skills may generalise. This is particularly likely since, as we describe below, these skills are not esoteric or specialised, but part of the normal repertoire of many positive teachers. If such skills can be developed, then this will be to the benefit of the teacher and colleagues as well as the referred pupil and the rest of the class. It will also be beneficial to all those children who will not subsequently be referred: that is, when such a teacher comes across difficulties of classroom disruption in the future, one may hope that he or she will be able to deal with them confidently without extensive external assistance, and without the possibility of children being referred to segregated provision. Thirdly, this type of intervention is

exceedingly cost-effective as it need not consume too
much of the team teacher's time. Given that the team
works to a hierarchy of intervention, then this method of working is a preferred option.

Having stressed the difficulties, the advantages
and the innovative nature of working with teachers,
it is now necessary to describe different ways of
working with them, and to elaborate more precisely
on the necessary skills and flexibility. This brings
us then to the subject of the title of this chapter
and, indeed, to one of the central contentions of
the book. If the argument of Chapter 1 is accepted,
that classroom disruption should be seen in a classroom context and not as a dimension of the personality of any of the participants, it follows that
changes in that context may be able to do much to
alter the pattern of disruption. As we have emphasised throughout, our notion of effective classroom
organisation is not based on any claim to esoteric
knowledge or skills, but on the systematic, positive
approach of many practising teachers (Leach D.J. and
Raybould, E.C., 1977).

The main concern of this section is with pedagogy, although we do conclude with some remarks on
the curriculum. Indeed, a main principle for avoid-
ing classroom disruption is to keep pupils busy with
curriculum work. Where teachers are approaching pupils with curriculum material which demands,excites and
challenges, there is less chance that they will need
to retreat with comments and complaints about behaviour. The curriculum demands obviously need to be
appropriate to the pupils in the group, but it is
also helpful to have a range of teaching styles and
tasks within any lesson. A varied sequence of activities helps to retain interest and momentum as well
as offering opportunities for different individual
skills. This, however, needs organisation and smooth
management. Pupils need to be told in advance how
the time is to be divided up, and transitions between tasks need to be handled smoothly and firmly.

Classroom rules should be precise and consis-
tent. It is probably best not to have unnecessary
rules: the fewer there are, the more likely they are
to be observed. What rules there are need to be understood by pupils and, if possible, endorsed by them
too. This tends to involve repetition with younger
children, and may well lead to a certain degree of
moral discussion with secondary classes. In both
cases this is probably educationally worthwhile as
well as being effective. This is not to say that ex-
ceptions cannot be made, but where this is done the

reasons need to be made clear to all the pupils.
Flexibility within a framework of consistency is
necessary with regard to both the curriculum and
standards of behaviour. The alternative can be a
series of unnecessary confrontations brought about
by the teacher's insistence that every child must
perform and behave up to some abstractly determined
set of standards.

A major element whereby a teacher can impart a
positive influence on lessons is by control of the
classroom environment (Coulby, D., 1984). Factors
within the teacher's control include the seating of
pupils and him/herself (who sits next to whom, the
size and arrangement of groups), displays on walls
and tables, the general tidiness and appearance of
the classroom, the positioning of equipment which
pupils are likely to use. Lack of time can make a
considerable impact on a lesson and they need to be
planned and adjusted according to the group and the
curricular material. A few minutes of routine activity at the beginning of a lesson can help to calm
a class after a hectic playtime. A dull and grumpy
class can often be improved by the even simpler ex-
pedient of opening a window. This concern for the
classroom environment should also include the physical organisation of lessons. Queues at a teacher's
desk are a further example of this. Many children
are probably wasting time in them, waiting instead
of working. They also block the teacher's vision and
attention from the rest of the class who are thus
more likely to stray from their tasks. The positioning of the teacher and the teacher's desk (is it
always necessary to have one?) are important, as is
freedom for the teacher to move effectively about
the classroom. The sedentary teacher can rarely be
as effective as one who spends at least some of the
time on the move. If the teacher is mobile in the
classroom, reading and attending to children's work,
initiating and contributing to discussion, praising
and encouraging good work and helping to resolve
difficulties, then the pupils are more likely to be
responding positively. Issues of the lesson can then
be dealt with before boredom or frustration compound
them into disruption. As an overall strategy, then,
it is better for the teacher to be approaching rather than retreating, better to be setting, super-
vising and assessing work than complaining about mis-
behaviour, better to be among the pupils' desks than
sitting behind one at the front of the room, better
to be aware of everything happening in the classroom
than being glued to one spot in the hope that every-

thing is going well elsewhere.

It is more effective to reward than to punish, and a readily available reward in the classroom is praise from the teacher. This is most effective when directed towards the details of academic performance; not just a vague "good", but a precise definition of what has been successfully achieved. The quicker the praise or any reward follows the successful performance, the more effective it is likely to be. More tangible rewards are available to teachers, such as allowing pupils time at preferred tasks or activities. Rather than a straight trade-off (teachers tend to shy away from anything that looks like a bribe), it may be preferable to reward a small group for the successful attainment, thereby gaining the support and encouragement of the group for the specified task. More detailed and programmed reinforcements are discussed later in this chapter, but at this stage it is worth noting that where tangible rewards are used, it may be necessary to offer some explanation to the rest of the class, though children are rarely unaware of the different personalities within their groups and the accordingly different demands these place on the teacher. Where this awareness appears to be lacking, or the singling out of a specific child even for reward seems to be inappropriate, it is possible to make a treat for the entire class contingent on successful performance by one child. Although group pressure may assist a teacher's aims in such a case, it is rather a strong force to call upon and may work against the long term interests of the pupil, either because it may subject him or her to undue pressure, or it may lead to the role of the class baby. Such procedures are best used with caution, and only when praise and encouragement have seemed to fail. If a team teacher were to suggest such a course to a class teacher, it is likely that the intervention would cease to be exclusively centred on the teacher. The team teacher would need to be more closely involved in the strategy as discussed below.

Inappropriate classroom behaviour may paradoxically be maintained by the teacher attention it generates, even where this is negative or actually punitive. At this stage matters become rather complex, and yet the policy (often recommended) of ignoring such behaviour is rarely practicable, and in a secondary classroom it could indeed prove disastrous. It may, however, be possible to minimise the attention received as a result of such behaviour. Quietly spoken, but firm, rebukes to individual pupils

are thought to be more likely to improve behaviour
than loud, public, negative comments. It is, however,
probably best for the teacher always to be seen to
be aware of what is going on in the classroom, and
to be seen to disapprove of what is not appropriate.
However, punitive methods rarely work unless they
form part of a well established pattern of reward and
punishment for which there is a strong consensus
amongst staff and pupils. In particular, corporal
punishment is not recommended. Apart from being in-
humane, it provides pupils with an undesirable example of violent authority. The fact that the same
pupils are often the recipients of repeated use of
corporal punishment is a testimony to its ineffect-
iveness. Other punishments are also going to run the
danger of becoming undermined by overuse or resentment if their effectiveness is not carefully moni-
tored. The most successful punishments are usually
those imposed in an atmosphere of reward, when it is
enough to punish by witholding reward. Other punishments - detentions or making good lost time or da-
mage - are probably more effective if they are not
delayed, if the pupil understands the reasons, and
if the teacher ensures that it is properly carried
out.

If appropriate curriculum and pedagogy are
used, it may be possible to avoid many confrontations, in which a teacher seeks recourse to threat
or punishment. Confrontations in the classroom are
an indication that inappropriate behaviour has become more important than the academic progress of
the lesson. However, if a confrontation with a pupil
has occurred, it is essential to spend some time
calming down afterwards, and to speak to the rest of
the class about it. If emotions remain high, chain
reactions of confrontations can occur. It may also
be helpful to see the individual pupil or pupils concerned later. It is tempting then to reason with
the pupil or extract promises, or to harangue them.
Unless this happens in the context of a strong positive personal relationship, it is likely to be
counter-productive. The reasons for this are that
the individual attention may actually be rewarding,
because that is the only form of individual attention
the pupil receives or, if it is definitely not rewarding, the pupil may say the right things simply
in order to get away. Instead, a brief but firm
statement of disapproval of the behaviour may be
enough. Some pupils may need the reassurance that
while the teacher may disapprove of the behaviour, he
or she does not dislike them as persons.

In case it should be thought that the team teacher only has to hand a distressed teacher a list of
the above do's and dont's of classroom management,
it ought to be stressed that these are principles
which they bear in mind. Most teachers know them in
any case, but some lack the confidence or opportunity to practise them. The team teacher's job is to
help the school teacher create the opportunity and to
encourage the gradual steps towards changes in practice.

The procedures of the team should help both the
school teacher and the team teacher to establish a
climate in which change can take place. The school
teacher has asked for some help with difficulties.
The team teacher asks the school teacher to do some
work by completing questionnaires and by discussion
in sharing in an assessment process. Usually the team
teacher will ask to do some classroom observation
and so gain first-hand experience of the context,
even if, as sometimes happens, the difficulties do
not appear so extreme during observation. The process
of assessment and, in particular, of feeding back
observations is vital. Firstly, it builds in a systematic and objective approach and, secondly, it is
gradual. We have already described the assessment
process in some detail and mentioned classroom observation as part of that process in Chapter 2. It
is rather the use that is made of certain kinds of
observation, and the nature of the feeding back, that
are important in working with teachers.

When feeding back, the team teacher needs to
make sure that there is something positive to say,
and to be entirely neutral in the way the difficult
events have been recorded. This is so much easier if
the class teacher has understood beforehand the nature of the observation and the method of recording.
For example, it may have arisen from the assessment
and formulation process, in which the class teacher
has shared, that one of the objectives for intervention was work on classroom management. The first step
in such an intervention may be to observe more closely what the pupil does, and how the teacher res-
ponds. This may take the form of a minute by minute
record over a fixed period of time, or something more
elaborate, with pre-designed codes for pupil behaviour (on task, looking, talking, movement, noise,
physical contact), and for teacher behaviour (teaching talk, controlling talk, praise, reprimand, mobi-
lity). Once the ideas behind systematic observation
have been grasped, there is no limit to the invention. Some teachers become adept at observing them-

selves (usually simple frequency counts of pupil behaviours). More important, the whole process sensiti-
ses them to observing informally, but more keenly, the
chain of reactions in their classroom. Once this happens
the team teacher may not need to continue classroom observation, and the class teacher may embark on a process
of change through regular discussions with the team teacher about his or her classroom practice, or rather the
particular aspects of it on which they are focusing.
Thus, the whole process is a mixture of a certain amount
of technique and method to which the team teacher has access, and a certain amount of support, in terms of two
people sharing a difficulty.

4.3 Work with teachers and individual pupils.

A much less complex way of working with teachers
in schools is to centre the intervention on an individual child. This is likely to be more acceptable to
teachers in school, as it does not assume that they play
any part in classroom disruption. Collaboration is then
all the easier. However, the benefits of working directly with teachers outlined in the preceeding section
are, in the main lost. Furthermore, this style of work
is a move towards focusing the blame as well as the
intervention on referred pupils. To a certain extent,
this difficulty is inherent within a mode of working
which is dependent on a referral system. On the other
hand, since the work is with teachers as well as children, it need not be quite as referral-centred as that
described in the next section.

One way of keeping the work's emphasis as being
that of collaborating alongside a teacher rather
than targeted at a pupil is to work in conjunction
with a particular teacher with a whole class. There
are several different ways in which this can be done
once the class teacher has accepted the invitation
to collaborate. One way is for the team teacher
simply to offer to take the class for a regular
session over a period of, say, a couple of weeks, to
give the class teacher a break. This might be appropriate where there was a high degree of disruption
and of teacher pressure. It certainly would provide
the team teacher with a sharp insight into what was
happening in the classroom. However, it has certain
disadvantages. If the team teacher is able to work
successfully with the class, then this is likely to
prove de-skilling to the classroom teacher. It may
become apparent to the class teacher, and perhaps
to the pupils also, that there is considerably less
disruption when the team teacher is taking the lesson. Since a main aim of the Unit's work is to de-

velop skills, flexibility and confidence among teachers, this would seem to be counter-productive. If the team teacher were to have as difficult a time with the class as their usual teacher, then it would be his or her position which would be undermined. This could hardly help the intervention, nor could the feeling, were it to develop among staff or pupils, that the class was becoming uncontrollable.

A more positive variation on this theme is effectively to reverse roles. Where a class teacher is insisting that it is just one or two children who are involved in disruption, that removing them from lessons would allow the others to proceed successfully, that this would also give the child or children some individual attention, it is possible to suggest that instead of the team teacher withdrawing the pupils, and the class teacher carrying on with the lessons, they simply change positions. The advantages here are quite profound. It is surely better for the pupils to form a positive, close relationship with a teacher in the school whom they are going to see a lot, rather than with a peripatetic teacher with whom contact is necessarily limited. The positive relationship idea might work both ways, and some individual time with the referred pupil(s) may help the class teacher to develop a more positive view of them and to understand in more detail their needs and capabilities. Furthermore, it may well be possible to reintegrate the referred pupil(s) back into the class quite easily as they will be going back alongside the class teacher. If the pupils had been withdrawn to be taught by the team teacher, there could well have been difficulties of reintegration. The only disadvantage of this method of work is that the team teacher is required to teach a class and probably a curriculum with which he or she is unfamiliar, and one which the class teacher is convinced will be free of disruption without the withdrawn pupils. It does require careful planning then and close collaboration over the curriculum.

Another method of working with pupils in cooperation with the class teacher is simply to team teach. This can be done either by both teachers circulating the whole class, or by one of them taking a small group within the context of the general lesson. The presence of two teachers is likely to diminish the opportunities for classroom disruption, and it may permit necessary attention and teaching time to be devoted to specific pupils who are likely to include those who have been referred. Team teaching also offers tangible support to class teachers within

the context where they consider themselves most to
need it. Where the class teacher is less experienced
than the team teacher at dealing with classroom disruption, it may provide opportunities for him or her
to learn some skills from the model of a colleague
actually in the same classroom. Since it is always
the class teacher who is in control of the curriculum and the structure of the lesson, then it is probable that the team teaching situation will not be
seen as a threat to his or her authority. Team teaching is a complex activity even in the best of circumstances so that, if it is to be attempted, it
does need some firm organisation in advance. For two
teachers to go into a lesson without having worked
out what their roles are going to be or without both
being familiar with the curriculum could well be a
recipe for disaster. Team teaching is an intervention which is quite costly in terms of time, since
it must continue over a period of at least weeks
(times and length of initial intervention being
agreed in advance), but it may be effective in that
it provides a tangible opportunity to assist both
pupils and teacher.

It may be possible to intervene more economi-
cally than this if both teachers can see the class
to have a conversation about classroom behaviour,how
it needs to be, and can be, improved. The presence
of a teacher from outside the school may provide a
suitably chastened atmosphere in which such a discussion can take place and can, indeed, lead to improvements. There is, however, the risk that in the
context, the team teacher will be perceived by the
pupils either as a bogey man or as some kind of authority figure with unknown powers. This would make
any further intervention either with the referred
pupil(s) or with the whole class more complicated.
As a way of persuading pupils seriously to address
the issue of behaviour it would not seem to have
many advantages over a similar discussion initiated
by, say, the class teacher and the head or deputy.
If planned in a more positive manner, however, and
if it is intended to lead to a further intervention
- say, to team teaching or to the group work described in a later section of this chapter - then it
may be a much more worthwhile process. It would, in
this case, allow the teachers to communicate their
views about what has been happening and what changes
they propose to make, and to hear the pupils' views
on these issues.

A final way in which class teacher and team teacher can collaborate in work with pupils is for the former to be involved in the work with individual referred pupils which is described in the next section. It may be essential to the success of an intervention for the class teacher to be involved in monitoring, rewarding and modifying any intervention and in explaining it to other teachers. It is desirable that the class teacher should be involved as closely as possible in the intervention, as without his or her co-operation it is unlikely to succeed. Furthermore, the team teacher will need eventually to taper and terminate the intervention, and one way of doing this is to hand it over to the class teacher. Again, close involvement of the class teacher in interventions with pupils is likely to develop his or her skills and confidence. It is highly desirable, then, that the education programmes, charts and contracts described below should be designed and implemented with the closest possible collaboration of class teachers.

4.4 <u>Work with individual pupils.</u>
In turning to work done with individual children, it is stressed that no-one has a monopoly on such work. The techniques described below can be used by teachers in mainstream schools. The peripatetic support team is only one way of making such services more available to teachers. The interventions described below could perhaps as easily be carried out by a specialist teacher within a school. They are indeed interventions which class teachers can and do learn themselves and subsequently use. As such they may form a useful practice to aid discussion.
At the basis of the team teachers' work with pupils is education and their skills in curriculum and pedagogy. Thus, if the decision is taken to remove a child from a class for certain times in the school week to be seen by the team teacher either individually or as part of a group, the bases of their contact is likely to be educational work. In some cases it may be found that the pupil has 'fallen behind' with a subject or has been at pains to acquire basic skills. Indeed, there could be a close relationship between academic frustration and involvement in classroom disruption. In these circumstances it could well be that some remedial help from the support teacher would help a successful reintegration back into class. Normally, the curriculum for such withdrawal sessions would be supplied by the class teacher, so the pupil retains contact with the

work of the rest of the class, but it may be appropriate sometimes to supplement this with material
designed or chosen by the team teacher. Even where
one of the objectives of the individual contact is
to form a relationship with a pupil and perhaps proceed to some educational guidance and counselling,
it is generally considered that this is best achieved
on the basis of some tangible educational work.

Even the most structured teaching, however, is
likely to lead to broader discussion when it is carried out on a one-to-one or small group basis. Educational guidance is likely to form part of this discussion. This can range from how to get on better in
Maths, to what options and exams to choose in the
fourth and fifth year. Some support teachers have
been trained as counsellors, and they may sometimes
make use of these skills with children. In these
cases, the educational and personal guidance may be
more formalised. The relationships team teachers develop with referred pupils are on the whole, however,
rather different from those favoured by the publi-
cists of school counselling. There is some risk in
making a mystique out of counselling. If it means
exploring with pupils issues wider than the formal
curriculum, giving them a sympathetic hearing, and
helping them to develop strategies to solve personal
problems, then many effective teachers were doing
this long before counselling was given diploma status.
Again, the aim of intervention is to share skills
with teachers and to exchange experience rather
than to attempt to transform it into an exclusive
domain. Nevertheless, counselling does have the advantage provided by more time and privacy which may
all help more intimate discussion. Of course, for a
child to discuss his or her problems is by no means
tantamount to their being solved, but it may be possible for the teacher and child at least to work out
what areas are beyond solution and what to do about
those that are not.

In fact, the notion of using the counselling
session to target on certain areas of behaviour is
fundamental to what is known as behavioural counselling. A distinction between that and client-centred counselling is necessary. In the latter the client sets the
theme of the discussion, and the counsellor reflects back feelings, contradictions, or diversions
in it. It requires a degree of self-awareness and
verbal fluency that is often lacking in a pupil whose
behaviour is disruptive. Behavioural counselling, however, takes as its focus the behaviour and not the
client. Since behaviour is public, for all to see,

then the counsellor may just as easily as the client
point out that certain people find certain behaviours
a problem. Of course, it is up to the client still
to decide whether to accept that, and whether it is
something on which he or she wants to work. Part of
the counsellor's work initially may be to build up
an awareness, through feeding back his or her own
observations and those of others, of what behaviour
is a problem and to whom, when, and how frequently,
it occurs. The more the pupil is able and willing to
take part in this information gathering, the more likely he or she will be to decide that alternative
ways of behaving may be worth considering. The techniques of behavioural counselling, therefore, are
those of behavioural analysis which have been described in the assessment stage of the team's work in
Chapter 2. The pupil learns how to analyse his or her
own behaviour, just as the teacher learns to analyse
the classroom situation.

It should be clear, therefore, that, from the
techniques of behavioural counselling, other more
specific interventions with individual pupils may
arise - the use of behaviour programmes, charts, contracts and social skills training. Indeed, these behavioural methods, all based on social learning
theory, far from being manipulations of the individual for social control, only really work when the
individual has been able to analyse his or her behaviour and fully agreed to work on certain aspects of
it. As long as the client is an active participant
in the analysis, it is academic whether behaviour
programmes are called behaviour modification. But it
is important that the analysis is thorough and the
programmes well carried out (Berger, M., 1979). The
basis of thorough behaviour analysis is observation.
The team teacher's observations may form the basis
of some discussion with individual pupils. Out of
that, they may decide to focus on one, two, or sometimes three classroom behaviours. The first stage in
this is often for the pupil to make his or her own
monitoring booklet in which the day or the week is
divided into appropriate time periods. As an initial
exercise, it may be best to start with a short period
(one hour) divided into short intervals (5 minutes).
If the interval is not less than about 15 minutes,
the teacher could be asked to find the time to record
with a tick or cross in the pupil's monitoring booklet, whether or not the target behaviours have occurred. These behaviours usually include doing something positive, e.g. on task, sitting still, completing work being quiet, etc., and refraining from

something negative, e.g. not shouting out, not running around, not fighting, etc. For shorter intervals, the task is too much for the teacher who is teaching at the same time, and so the pupil can monitor himself or herself, or arrange with other pupils for them to do so. If a reciprocal monitoring system can be worked out, it is amazing how accurate and dedicated pupils can be. Another monitoring system that has been tried is a combination of self-monitoring (most of the time) and teacher monitoring (occasionally). Whatever the results of the observations, it is best if the pupil's observations agree with the teacher's. Then praise for their accuracy and honesty is stressed. After this initial stage of monitoring, the team teacher and the pupil can set targets for the next few days or weeks to increase the frequency of some behaviours or reduce others. The pupil may need some specific reward for achievement (an opporunity to do something special, a visit by someone, a visit out, a reward for the whole class, a letter home, extra time with certain activities), but always praise and sometimes only praise. On the subject of rewards, each pupil is different, and they will soon find what suits them best. The younger child will need more frequent rewards and a chart, which is a method of visibly plotting progress towards a reward, may be the best method (see below).

The object of rewards, however, is that as appropriate behaviour becomes more frequent, it will bring its own natural rewards - the satisfaction of achievement, the approval of others - and the need for special rewards will diminish. That is why the essence of a behaviour programme should aim to increase appropriate behaviour and not just decrease inappropriate behaviour. Sometimes, when the curriculum is inappropriate for the child, the opportunity for appropriate behaviour may be limited.

The principles and practice of behaviour programmes have been well described elsewhere (Harrap, A., 1983, Lane, D., 1978a, 1978b, Wheldall, K. [Ed.], 1981). Although they are an important part of many interventions, it is the flexibility to adapt support to the climate of a particular school and the needs of a particular situation that we wish to emphasise in this chapter. Other behavioural techniques include charts, behaviour contracts, and social skills training. Charts have the attraction of engaging the pupil's imagination and creative ability, as well as reasoning, in the process of change. The chart is a visual representation of a pupil's progress towards a behavioural goal. It is helpful to take a child's

interest (e.g. football, fishing, animals, super-
heroes, computers) and help him or her to design and
make a chart. Examples that we have seen include
filling in one segment of web by Spiderman for every
10 minute period working, completing stages of a
rocket for Star Wars, hooking paper fish out of a
three-dimensional model of a river, filling in scales
of a snake skin with the reward of someone bringing
a live python to school. The activity itself of completing some of the more ingenious charts can be a
sufficient reward. Sometimes, the chart is a private
matter between the child and the team teacher, sometimes shared with a class teacher, and sometimes the
sole responsibility of the class teacher. If the chart
is public to the class, other pupils may want one.
The solution to this is either to build a class reward into the individual chart, or to give those who
want one a chart. Those who actually need one will
benefit, those who do not really need one will usually not ask for a second.

Behaviour contracts are an extension of charts
in some ways, except that they move from a mainly
visual to a mainly verbal format, and in that sense
may be more likely to appeal to the older child. A
contract is simply an agreement that if the child
does X, the adult will do Y. It is making clear the
connection between two behaviours and making one dependent on the other (Homme, L., 1969). When a contract is kept, it teaches a child two things: firstly, that the adult's behaviour does depend on his or
hers, and secondly, that adults do what they say
they are going to do. Thus, the behaviour in the contract is reinforced and keeping a contract is reinforced. If the contract is not completed successfully, this is regarded as a failure of the contract
(as, indeed, it is - the whole point of drawing them
up is that they should work), and not of the pupil:
this means that an alternative more feasible document can then be drawn up. Sometimes a pupil may progress from one contract onto several others - usually
either more demanding or extending over more time.
Though, as with all such programmes, the most definite reward that pupils receive is more positive
access to their curriculum and the raised esteem of
teacher and (hopefully) peers. Everyone is rewarded
by having classrooms which are appreciably less disrupted.

Beyond these interventions in schools, the Unit
has recourse to placing individual secondary aged
children part-time and for a short specified period
in its own class. This is not to say that involvement

with the school and the class teachers ceases at this
point. Pupils usually attempt to follow their mainstream school curriculum whilst at the Unit. It is,
therefore, necessary to keep close contact with the
school, so that the class teacher is informed of the
curriculum and provided with the relevant materials.
The teacher of the Unit's class may well make contact with the school in addition to their usual team
teacher in discussions before placement. Likewise,
the team works during the time the pupil is at the
Unit to ensure that reintegration can go ahead without difficulties. It is rarely wise to return a pupil back into the context where there has previously
been disruption. Attempts are often made to change
curriculum, class groups, subject teachers, or staff
attitudes towards a pupil before he or she returns
to his or her school full-time. Paradoxically then,
when a pupil is placed in the Unit's class, this may
actually involve more contact with the school rather
than less.

A curricular element which team teachers do
frequently add to the education of young pupils concerns social skills training. The idea behind this
is that behaviour causing trouble in school may result from lack of skill in social interaction - e.g.
in asking for something, or in conveying anger without violence. A socially skilled person can influence
their social interactions to bring about a rewarding
outcome. The aim in social skills teaching is to
teach 'getting on with people' as a collection of
skills with the intention of enabling pupils to increase the range and quality of their social interactions. It has recently earned rather an unfortunate reputation for itself, as it has become a component of YTS courses (Bash, L. et al, 1985). There
is genuine and justifiable anxiety lest social skills
training be a direct form of social control and manipulation of young people, teaching them how to be
subservient and uncomplaining wage fodder.

This may be countered by discussing the content
of the social skills session with the pupils beforehand. They can, first of all, identify through small
group work and personal questionnaires their own
areas of skill and deficiency. They can then determine what skills, either related to school or to the
wider world, they think that it would be helpful to
learn. The analysis of social skills which we have
found the most useful involves 'micro' or basic
skills and 'macro' or complex skills. Thus, qualities
like eye contact, posture, voice quality, and perception of facial expressions are micro skills. More

complex interactions like apologising, making friends
in a new place, temper control, collaborating, are
macro skills.

Each session follows a broadly similar pattern:
introduction of theme, instruction and discussion,
modelling of behaviour, practice and feedback. All
the work is done in small groups of no more than
eight. The theme is often a macro skill within which
one or two micro skills may be picked out for certain individuals. The pupils are then encouraged to
discuss the theme as fully as possible, to analyse
the component skills and how they differ according
to the situation. Sometimes, in the course of discussion, aspects of behaviour are discussed which
may call for some instruction, e.g. to become more
aware of bodily tension. The group can then decide
what particular skill is to be taught in relation to
the theme that they have discussed. The next stage
is for the teacher to ask one of the pupils to model
the skill, to demonstrate its use, in a brief role-
play if necessary. The advantage of a small group is
that different pupils will have different needs and
will be able to model skills for one another. If this
is not possible, video material may be used, but it
is best if it is a recording of someone they like and
respect. The group is then asked to practise the
skill in question, usually in small groups of two or
three, using exercises like scripted or unscripted
role-plays or a task whose completion is only possible if the skill is used. A video camera is often
available, and some of the pupils may wish to film
one another during this practice. The video can then
be used, with the pupils' permission, during the
feedback at the end when the practice is discussed.
Each person is invited to give positive comments on
their own and others' performances.

This style of work is clearly a bit strange to
some pupils, if they are not used to open discussion
about other people in front of them, or to learning
from one another rather than from the teacher. In
practice we have found that the sessions run better
with two teachers, so that the pupils can see the
two teachers discussing with one another as members
of the group and changing roles from instructor to
participant. Usually, pupils attend social skills
for a series of sessions, the number of which is
usually between six and ten, but agreed at the outset.

4.4.1 Illustrative material: An interview with a team teacher.

Int One of the things that interests me most is the charts that you did largely with pupils in primary schools. These are very vivid and colourful, and seem to have lots of inventive ideas that are geared into the level of the children with whom you were working. How did this graphically imaginative work form part of what you were doing with referred children?

TT When I started going round the schools I felt very much that I was just a person coming to talk, and sometimes that kids thought I was somebody who was coming to talk about a problem. And I felt very unexciting. So then I started to take things with me. And I knew that in classrooms there are some things that are held at a premium, like exciting 3D pop-up or generally informal type books and new felt tips in bold colours, etc. So I always carried things like that with me, and I developed a style whereby, especially when I didn't know a kid very well, I just shared something and we got involved in that. And then I'd start branching out and asking about things from there rather than going straight in as a stranger and saying "Right, this is what I've been told you do."

Int You mean, "This is what I've been told you do wrong?"

TT Yes. So still when I'm brought a child who's done something inappropriate, I often start off by saying, "Did you go swimming last week (as you planned)?" Because if you just start on why they've been brought to you, which is something negative, then they'll close up.
    So, I had all this paper and really nice pens and I must have been attracted to the idea of charts. I liked the idea of making things really eye-catching and bright. And although I prefer kids to do their own drawing, they like it if you do drawings for them too. If we were short of time I'd whip up something that impressed them. But it would be motivated from something we'd been talking about, so it would often come from the chat, not from the so-called problem.

Int So mention some of the things that you used for the charts that came from the chat.

TT Something that the kid wanted for Christmas – "I'd like to go to a pantomime" or "to have a science experiment kit." And so the chart would be the child with a most amazing science experiment kit, opening it on Christmas day. So, in lots of ways it was nothing to do with the behaviour you were trying to change.

Int It was to do with motivation.

TT Well, not necessarily. Sometimes it would just be that the kid was absolutely crazy about <u>Star Trek</u>.

Int So you used that as a way of keying in the interest and providing rewards for appropriate behaviour?

TT Yes, probably. And also, because the chart was such a public thing, it drew attention to what that child liked. This child had a picture of himself and one of the main characters from <u>Star Trek</u> on the (classroom) wall.

Int So that was the reinforcement?

TT Yes. I guess so.

Int In the records you can find ten different charts that you did with one child or twenty with another. Would you describe one particular case.

TT The referral was because of "the problem family". The child had been moved about a bit, and his parents were separated. In school, I tied the referred behaviour down to not knowing how to be friendly with other children. The teachers said he wanted contact with other children but he could only get it negatively, so every playtime, every lunchtime, and occasionally in class, he was in trouble with other kids.

Int And you perceived this as a lack of skill in <u>making</u> friends rather than a negative capacity?

TT I thought you could teach him how to make and keep friends. The other thing was it did spill over into the classroom and affected the teacher's attitude to the child. He was thought of as "aggressive". And, because he didn't get on with children he sat next to, it meant he rarely settled in his work.

Int So it was more a matter of the child's relation to his peer group than his relationship with the teacher?

TT Yes.

Int So you decided to work on the basis of encouraging him to make positive friendships?

TT The starting point was, I said to him "If I was your really best mate, what sort of things would you like me to say to you?" And he really couldn't say. He had no idea. So I used to practise saying "I really like sitting next to you. You're fun to sit with". He said he was going just to experiment with that, and I left it very informal. And I think, in a way, it wasn't structured enough, so I decided, at this point, to start using the charts. I also felt that he ought to have some sort of structure for receiving rewards from the peer group. In the end I brought in a ball. I found out that in the playground a ball was a big prize, and so I brought him a ball. Then every playtime he had children who would come and play with him.

He had a chart that said something like, "this week I'm going to play football with my friends in the playground". There'd be lots of windows (on the chart) which would open, and every day he would write in the name of someone he'd played football with. The next week we had another chart where people who played with him signed a football. And that went up on the wall.

Then we started branching out and having pictures of anything. He really liked Illya who is a character in <u>Star</u> <u>Trek</u>. He described her, and I had a go at drawing her. He was really pleased with this picture and could see himself alongside this heroine on the wall for all to see. On this chart he would then himself fill in how he had got on in the lunchtime and at breaktime. Sometimes the lunchtime supervisors would be asked to add comments each day. At the end of the day, if there were more good comments than bad, he would colour in a starship.

Gradually he started to get good comments all the time for his breaks and lunchtimes, so the charts also took on a role of being a proclamation as well. Part of it would say "Well done (Clive) for having such a wonderful week last week." But specifying exactly <u>how</u>: e.g. "I played with so many children", or "the lunchtime supervisors were really pleased with me for taking turns with Tariq and Polly."

Int To reinforce him in specific ways and also draw the attention of members of staff.

TT Yes, but also other children too.

Int Without the evaluative data, how do you judge your effectiveness in this case?

TT Well, partly by what the child was saying. Partly the fact that teachers would greet me with smiles and say "This is wonderful". However, it was a bit of a "yes - but" thing with the teacher. When the referred playground behaviour had been sorted out,it then became, "Oh, his behaviour is fine in the playground, and he's more friendly in the classroom, but he still doesn't do as much work as the other children." I decided, seeing as how he was doing so well, I would actually carry on for a while. And he wanted it, and he really used to look forward to his hour on his own with me once a week.

Int Yes. It was a maintenance thing.

TT He would talk non-stop about himself and how wonderfully he was getting on, and so on. As time went on, I wanted to make the charts different. You didn't just want a picture of somebody every week, and somewhere for him to talk. So we started to do things like write letters to people. Say the letter was to someone he'd find rewarding, like the head teacher, it would be "Dear (head teacher) I have been friendly all week". He would get one word in the letter ready twice a day. When the words were cut out and ready, then he would just stick one on. Then, on the last day, he'd deliver it round. The head teacher would be prepared with a nice reaction about how wonderful this was, and perhaps even show the letter in assembly. As this went on, we then got onto cumulative charts. So, as one example, he had a helicopter - he'd seen a programme or something, and was crazy about them that week. The propellers moved round revealing a different day, and on the outside were the sections: - morning, lunchtime, afternoon. It was a straight maintenance thing really. He just had to do something friendly three times every day. But it was very exciting to move it on to the next day. And also there were spaces at the bottom for comments of praise by the teacher about pieces of good work. Every day it would say "Did well in reading today", or "Worked well

I can catch my te...

(whenever I want to!)

Friday!

Monday Tuesday Wednesday Thursday

Every day I keep my temper I will move it
along, until I get to Friday, then I close the cage door!

CLIVE.

CLIVE SUPPORTS ARSENAL.

EACH DAY WHEN **CLIVE** BEHAVES WELL HE SCORES
A GOAL FOR ARSENAL. — IF BY A MIRACLE HE DOES
SOMETHING WHICH ISN'T GOOD BEHAVIOUR HE SCORES
A GOAL FOR WEST HAM! BOO!!
IF TERRY LOSES HIS TEMPER
THAT ALSO SCORES A GOAL
FOR ARSENAL.

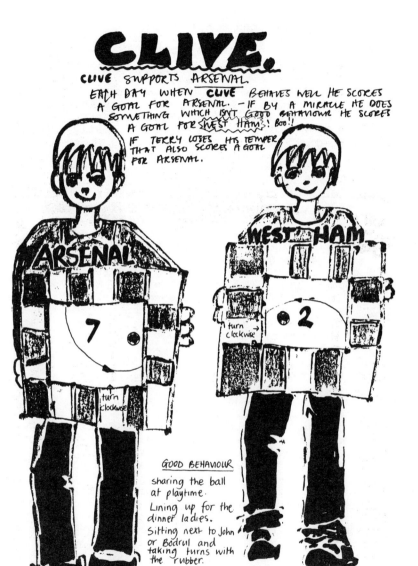

GOOD BEHAVIOUR

sharing the ball
at playtime.

Lining up for the
dinner ladies.

Sitting next to John
or Bodrul and
taking turns with
the rubber.

Being nice and friendly
to all my friends.

and did some good art."

Int What part in the child's improved behaviour do you think was played specifically by his work with charts?

TT The child had to find the charts rewarding for a start. And you knew straight away whether they would. The only way to make the charts rewarding was to get to what the child was really interested in. The charts forced the support teacher to become involved in what motivated the child. So that during the hour you spent with him you talked about all the things he loved to talk about as much as about his behaviour. That in itself was a reward. He looked forward to seeing you when you came. The brightness attracted attention, adults immediately walked over to the board and said "What's this?" The name was bold and clear. The achievements so far were bold and clear. And it gave you a way of working with the teacher while the teacher felt the focus was on the child. It even allowed teachers who quite resisted it at first to focus on the positive. It was also advertising their achievement. But it was especially a nice way of including the peer group.

4.5 Work with pupils and their families.

The thinking and rationale behind the team and its way of working indicate a preference to locate difficulties of classroom disruption within the school rather than ascribe it to the family of the pupil concerned. This is not to say, however, that family dynamics or forms of deprivation at home do not affect the behaviour of pupils in school. Other professionals - social workers or child guidance personnel - may be in a better position to help families in such difficulties. But, a great deal does depend on the kind of relationship that a school has with its parents. To this extent a team teacher can help the school to enlist parental support for the educational endeavours in school.

Sometimes, school and the parents of a child are in conflict, or communication has broken down. Each starts to blame the other for the child's behaviour, or each thinks that the other is about to act accusingly. Whatever the origin of such a conflict, it is not an atmosphere in which the child can receive clear messages about what is expected in school. Evidence (Central Advisory Council for Education, 1964, etc.) suggests that parental support

for school is an important factor in determining a
child's academic progress. In all cases, where the
team teacher works directly with the individual child
(as opposed to just teachers or a group of children),
the school is expected to inform the parents. When
this happens, the team teacher will usually ask someone in the school who knows the parents already to
arrange for them to meet. This will either happen in
school or a home visit will be made. In fact, the
active support of parents is sought by team teachers
for 25% of the children referred to the Schools Support Unit.

This type of contact with parents is one of
sharing a school problem with them, and of explaining the nature of support that the team teacher is
hoping to give the school. Although some parents may
be hesitant, or even hostile at first to the idea of
extra help of this nature for their child in school,
it is fair to say that patient explanation and persistence have always won them over. The majority of
parents are only too pleased, and they readily offer
practical help. This help may take several forms.
It may involve approving of a reward, or giving a
reward to a pupil for certain changes in behaviour
that the pupil is trying to achieve in school. The
best reward is the undivided attention that the parents give to the child in noticing something worthy
of approval. This attention is guaranteed if the parents have agreed to read and sign a daily or weekly
monitoring booklet, or to fill in a chart which the
pupil brings home.

A simpler kind of arrangement with parents, but
one which may take just as much trouble to set up,
is to get them and the school to agree on exactly
what behaviour in school would leave the school no
option but to inform the parents. Sometimes parents
get so used to letters from school, informing them
of their child's difficult behaviour, that either
they start to ignore them, or else they go on the
offensive and begin to feel that their child is being
unjustly treated. A more effective agreement still
with parents is to decide how parents will react
with their child if there is bad news from the school.
Most of this sort of work centres around making sure
that different people have the same understanding
about why they are communicating with one another.
Sometimes, it helps in early stages of new agree-
ments and understandings to get the precise expectations written down in the form of a contract (see
above) to be signed by all parties, including the
child.

Once a basis of trust between home and school is established, more positive contacts are likely to succeed and informal communication can take place directly between the parents and the teachers, without the mediation of the team teacher. Parents have begun to feel less threatened about going into schools and, therefore, less likely to stay away, or to go in and take the offensive, which is the other side of the same coin. Schools, too, have learned to share more easily with parents, encouraged no doubt by both national and local reports of committees of enquiry. Teachers have begun to find that there is a place for parents in school, not tucked away in a parents' room, but in the classroom as extra helpers. The process in general is a slow one, but with certain individual parents the transformation can be extremely rapid. It is not unknown for the most hostile parents to turn within a year into the ones who, almost single-handedly, rejuvenate the defunct PTA.

Finally, there is an aspect of work with parents that does focus on problems that they as parents may be having at home with their child or children. The focus shifts from school to home or stays on both simultaneously, because, perhaps, parents begin to feel that the school shares its responsibility with them for the child's behaviour at school. The parents place confidence in the school and the team teacher and may be more willing to talk about domestic problems. The team teachers have to keep a sense of proportion. They cannot take on financial or housing worries that a parent may bring to them, but they can refer them to an appropriate agency. In conjunction with other professionals - educational psychologists, child guidance, education welfare officers - they can help the parents with the behaviour problems that the children present to them. Clearly, the same kind of systematic behaviour analysis can be applied in the home as in the classroom and the level of support has to be as intense, too. Some parents do well on that kind of short-term practical support, others do well on the family therapy approach favoured by many child guidance centres. The team's education welfare officer and team teachers have set up and led groups for parents both during the day and in the evenings, in schools and in adult education institutes, so that they can discuss behaviour problems that they have with their children.

These interventions, however, are not tried with parents on a cookbook basis. They only work if

the assessment shows that domestic problems are
likely to be contributing to, or maintaining, the
child's behaviour problems. They only work if both
the child and the parents have a shared understanding of what the difficulties are, and a motivation
to do something about it. Even then, the emphasis
of the support team is to support the school and
to maintain the best possible provision that the
school can make to meet the child's needs.

4.5.1 Illustrative material: Olu.

This case illustrates a team intervention within a family. Olu was a fourteen-year-old boy in a
comprehensive school. He was the oldest of four
children in a West African family who came to Britain
to further their education. They intend to return to
Africa at some point. When Olu was referred to the
Schools Support Team, the reason for referral was
given as:

(1) outbursts of physical and verbal aggression;
(2) lack of progress;
(3) speech and communication problems.

A number of interventions were attempted within the
school with some moderate success.

Assessment and formulation.

Analysis of the factors within the home influencing
Olu's school behaviours revealed an isolated family,
over-anxious about Olu's potential academic attainment. They were extremely concerned that their son
should not get in trouble on the streets. Significantly, the parents allocated a large amount of household
tasks such as washing, ironing and cooking to the
boy for which he received no recognition from them,
either in the form of praise or time out in the evenings. In consequence, he exploited the comparatively
liberal environment which he experienced at school
by periodically creating difficulties for staff
and other pupils.

Intervention.

The Senior Education Welfare Officer and team teacher
worked jointly with the family over a long period.
An agreement was eventually negotiated where the family would allow Olu out to a supervised youth club
on selected evenings; this being conditional upon
positive behaviour reports from school. Additionally,
with a great deal of encouragement, Olu's father was
able to praise his son and speak positively in his

presence. The joint intervention brought about a significant improvement in Olu's behaviour, although minor problems occasionally arose.

4.6 Work with groups of pupils.

A development that has gradually gathered momentum within the team's work has been work with groups of pupils. Initially, this always arose out of the referral of an individual pupil. In such a case, the assessment period would show up that the pupil had social difficulties in a group which the group were playing a part in maintaining. Most pupils referred present social problems in groups but, in some cases, the group was seen to be contributing to the problem as much as the pupil. Therefore, it was clear that intervention would have to focus on the group as well as on the pupil, or even perhaps not on the pupil at all. Such a pupil may otherwise be identified as the class scapegoat or clown or bully. The observer of the group might almost be inclined to say that, even if the referred pupil were removed, another pupil from the group would quickly emerge to play that role.

In time, schools have become more confident in identifying a problem as a group problem, and in sharing that with someone from outside. A formal process now exists for schools to refer groups, classes, or whole years. This is a considerable change of emphasis from referring an individual pupil, since it actually implies that the school recognises that any responsibility for the state of affairs must be located within the school and not within the child or within the family.

The process of working with a group, whether referred as such or arising from an individual referral, is similar to that of working with an individual. Emphasis is placed on assessment and on sharing a formulation with participants. Assessment mainly takes the form of observation, although sometimes some sociometric questionnaires to pupils are useful. The observations take note of how pupils group themselves, who interacts with whom, who initiates activities, who follows, and who deviates, what results from these actions, and what effect the consequences have on them. All of this then is fed back to the teacher(s) and, if possible, to the pupils. In the course of observations, pupils will inevitably ask the observer what he or she is doing. The experienced observer will answer truthfully, without giving a full history of the referral. Other questions may arise and, by the time the observations are finished, the group will probably be aware that people are interested in how they get on with one another. The feedback of observations should, therefore, be not too much of a surprise to pupils, and may be seen as coming from someone who is no longer regarded as a total stranger.

Sometimes a group is perceived to have a cohesive core of pupils who are finding it difficult to adapt to new members, or to new teachers. In these cases, particularly in secondary schools, the group may have enough strength to be able to act on the feedback without special intervention. Periodic observation and feedback may be sufficient to reinforce the changes that the group has been able to make spontaneously. At other times, a group seems to lack cohesion, or to have constantly changing roles and patterns of friendship, or to feel threatened by attempts at leadership by the teacher. This may require a more formal intervention which sets up communications so that the group members can start to inform one another about themselves. The observations may have shown that certain skills were not being used, such as listening or co-operating, or that certain issues were being constantly brought up, but never resolved, such as feeling unfairly treated in comparison to other groups, or feeling insecure because of recent traumatic experiences of one or two members of the group.

The intervention has then consisted of planning with a teacher or teachers in the school a series of regular sessions with the group. Whatever the purpose of the whole series, the sessions nearly always will include communication games. These involve games, sometimes paper and pencil, sometimes purely verbal, sometimes purely non-verbal, in which the group is split up into smaller subgroups or pairs, and some problem has to be solved or discussed. The solutions are then brought back to the main group. The problem may be just fun - e.g. one pupil is given a complex shape to describe, but not to show to a partner who then has to draw it. It may be a real problem - e.g. how the group is going to receive a visitor to the class the following week. The aim of the sessions is to set up pairings and subgroups on different combinations, and to encourage sharing information with the whole group. They aim to build up channels of communication between group members and to develop mutual respect and trust.

Working with groups brings in many other aspects of school organisation that need careful advance planning. Firstly, there is the question of how the

sessions are fitted into the timetable and that, in
a secondary school, may interfere with the curriculum
of a particular department. Therefore, the team teacher often has to involve heads of department as well
as pastoral staff in setting up the sessions. When
the sessions are running, what does the teacher who
usually takes that class do? Ideally, that teacher
should run the session jointly, but he or she may not
feel trained in such group techniques, or not want to
participate as anything but a trained teacher. But
these problems may show up a need within the school,
which can be discussed with staff. Working with groups
has often led team teachers into far-reaching discussions about ways in which school curriculum, timetabling or school organisation may predispose disruptive behaviour. In some cases, they have been invited to take part in looking at some of these areas
more closely and at in-service training for staff in
schools. Some of these exciting forms of collaboration are discussed in more detail in the next chapter.

4.6.1 <u>Illustrative Material: Interview with a team
teacher about a group referral.</u>

Int Let's start at the beginning. How did the referral of a group of pupils originate?

TT A year tutor was concerned about a specific child,
but she was not convinced that it was appropriate
to refer him because she thought that the peer
group was unduly influencing him. So I asked if
it would be fairer to look at the whole group
first.

Int So how did you establish a reason for referral?

TT I asked the year tutor to call a meeting of the
group's subject teachers, and from that discussion we agreed that the reason was too much noise
and an incohesive group.

Int O.K. So, then you were able to start some assessment?

TT Yes. I asked my colleague, the other team teacher who works in the school, to help me with
some class observations. We did some observations together, and some separately.

Int That sounds interesting. What happened next?

TT We fed back the observations to the group of subject teachers. Having two of us helped them to
see our observations as valid. Of course, we had

some differences, but our general impressions and frequency counts of various behaviours were pretty similar. We found the pupils to be a very bright group, with a lot of energy, very noisy and needing a lot of structure. We identified a smaller group of seven or eight who seemed to be at the centre of things. We also saw certain individual pupils with specific needs, who might need some support for learning, but not necessarily from the Support Unit. Teachers again mentioned the noise, and also some racist incidents. One teacher, in particular, made a lot of complaints about the group.

Int Right. So far, you have made observations and used those to try and get the teachers to think about the group's behaviour. Did you arrive at any formulation of the problem?

TT Yes. We tried to go for one with the teachers. We weren't quite sure what the dynamics of the group were, but we thought that we needed something to go on, to try out.

Int O.K. I know you may be tentative about it, but I would still like to hear it.

TT Well, we felt that the group was bright and energetic, and that the noise was partly a product of a lack of structure in the lessons, and partly the product of them using the free space resulting from that to work out their rather complicated dynamics. By structure, we meant the pupils individually or in groups knowing what to go on to when the task was finished. Also, one specific lesson was in the teacher's own words a 'regular disaster', and this spilt over into surrounding lessons.

Int That was quite a lot to deal with. What did you do?

TT We decided to concentrate on just one thing first. We felt that one particular subject-area should be tackled. We planned with the teacher to take one of the lessons he taught once a week for five weeks, and that we would go through group exercises to allow the group to look at their friendship patterns and communications. This involved some role-play, some writing-completing questionnaires, some communication games, and as an end product some video of the group playing the games, which was really to give them some feedback. Each session ended with a fun exercise for which the teacher came in to participate. Fortunately, we had kept the head of department informed all along, and he squared it with the head.

Int How did the pupils respond to you as new teachers when previously they had only seen you as observers?

TT Well, I suppose they put us on trial, but they enjoyed what we did. It was a bit difficult when they started making remarks to us about other teachers, but I suppose that is always going on in schools. There was a crucial time, when we noticed that one member of the group was being scapegoated. It was almost a ritual. We decided to point it out to them, and we said that we weren't going to do anything about it - it was up to them. We didn't see any more of it.

Int That does sound important, but I wonder what effect this was having on other teachers at the time, and what happened after the five weeks had finished?

TT In between times, I spent a lot of time with the teacher whose lesson we took. I just gave him attention and tried to get him to think through his ideas. We did not have a formal review of the work. Perhaps we should have done. We had lots of informal chats with other teachers who were more positive about the group. The Head of Year reported 50% fewer complaints, and started to arrange for extra learning support from the special needs department for three pupils whom we had previously identified. One other pupil now stood out as having persistent problems of controlling his behaviour, and I agreed to work with him in the usual way.

Int Well, thank you very much. The main thing that strikes me is that it must take a lot of trust between you and the teachers for them to want you to do work like that. But the pay-offs seem to be as great as the trust.

Chapter 5

SCHOOL ORGANISATION

5.1 School Organisation and Disruptive Behaviour.

The link between the organisation of a school and
the disruptive behaviour of specific pupils (made in
Chapter 1) is easier to assert than to specify. It
has been suggested (Rutter, M. et al., 1979) that,
even controlling for such factors as socio-economic
background or the attainment level of children at
the time of entry into different schools, there are
significant differences between secondary schools in
terms of the behaviour of their pupils. It was argued that these differences were connected with the
organisation or, less tangibly, the ethos of the
school.

School organisation implies those activities that
teachers and ancillary staff carry out in order to
construct situations in which learning can take place.
Such a behavioural account would place little emphasis on ethos, rather it would suggest a long list of
activities as varied as cleaning the school, check-
ing attendance of pupils, and chairing meetings about
the curriculum. This account would see organisation
as a process of getting people, largely in groups,
to be in certain places, at certain times, in a certain sequence. However, even if all the activities
of school organisation could be specified, it would
still need to be acknowledged that a further important variable would be the spirit in which these tasks
were carried out. A highly efficiently organised
school in which people communicated in a cynical or
apathetic way might well generate disruptive behaviour by alienating pupils. It is, then, necessary
to see school organisation and school ethos as being
inseparable, despite the unfortunate vagueness of
the notion of ethos. Nevertheless, there may be certain key activities that predispose people to com-

municate in particular ways, or certain ways of communicating that predispose certain forms of organisation. The search for these particular philosopher's stones is not likely to proceed by statistical analysis alone, but also by the careful ordering and evaluation of experience.

Aspects of school organisation which might be linked with pupil behaviour include:-

1. school rules and the way in which they are applied;
2. timetabling, movement about the school, and arrangements for lunchtimes and breaks;
3. the responsibilities that teachers have towards one another and towards different groups of pupils;
4. the communication system of the school, particularly the reliability and accuracy of the information about pupil behaviour that is passed from one teacher to another;
5. the nature of teachers' contacts with parents;
6. the in-service training and support offered to teachers.

This chapter will proceed through these six points in turn. In this way, it will be seeking to achieve two separate objectives: firstly, to emphasise the importance of school organisation on the generation of classroom disruption; secondly, to indicate ways of intervening in a school organisation which might serve to reduce the frequency of disruptive incidents. The illustrative material provides examples of some of the ways in which the Support Unit has attempted to make such interventions.

The Support Unit has been involved in aspects of school organisation both intentionally and incidentally. Intentional involvements such as observations, in-service training, or parents groups were established as discrete projects at the initiative of either the school or the team. It is less easy to describe or evaluate the incidental influence in any one school. Someone visiting a school frequently over a long period in order to help with disruptive behaviour is likely to establish a position of some influence. The presence of an outsider directing a good deal of energy to examining practices within a school may prompt teachers within the school to reflect on their own organisational procedures. Discussions with the support teacher are then likely to form one aspect of this reflection.

Some research carried out within the team
(Harper, T., 1984) indicated the importance of
school organisation as a factor in disruptive activity. In this study (which was described in more
detail in Chapter 3) three groups of pupils were
followed from their fourth year in junior school to
the end of their first year in secondary. The groups
consisted of pupils showing disruptive behaviour referred to the team, pupils showing disruptive behaviour not referred, and pupils showing no disruptive behaviour. The biggest shift in behaviour of all
three groups occurred after transfer between schools
and not after any change of teacher. This may have
been partly due to the fact that in the first year
of secondary school they were the youngest in a
school, whereas in the fourth year of junior school
they were the oldest. Interviews with the pupils
concerned, however, suggested that they were more
influenced by the strangeness of their new school
in the beginning of the first year than about their
status in the peer group. Organisational factors may
well have influenced the changes in behaviour.

5.2 School Rules.

An interesting aspect of school rules is that it
often takes a long time for someone to find out what
the real rules are. Often there are two sets of
rules. One set is formal, and may be periodically
announced or written down. The second set are those
which can only be found if a pupil pushes someone
too far, or if a teacher needs to invoke legitimation for anger or rash actions provoked by the irritating behaviour of pupils. These are the implicit
rules which are constantly negotiated and re-interpreted through action rather than formal announce-
ment.

There is obviously a need for formal school
rules to ensure safety, co-operative behaviour, the
safekeeping of the school and its contents, the
avoidance of racist or sexist behaviour. These rules,
however, should be kept to the minimum. Unnecessary
rules, or ones the pupils can legitimately dispute,
are likely to bring all the rules, including the essential ones, into disrepute. The rules need to be
known to pupils and discussed with them. The rules
are more likely to be obeyed if pupils have had the
opportunity to question them and thereby to understand why they are necessary. Of course, if the pupils manage to prove that some rules are not necessary, then it would probably be appropriate to drop
them. The aim of rules, after all, is not to inspire

blind obedience, but rather to develop in children
and young people qualities of self-discipline and
co-operation. This is much more likely to be achieved
by rules which are known, understood, discussed, and
endorsed than by a long list of largely unnecessary
restrictions which are unquestioningly enforced and
obeyed.

Another reason for keeping school rules brief
and open to discussion is that this is likely to
lead to some agreement among members of staff. A
hazardous situation in a school occurs when not
all the staff endorse all the rules. It then becomes
difficult for some teachers to enforce rules which
they actually think are unnecessary or excessively
rigid. When this occurs the school no longer has a
coherent policy, as pupils will behave in one way
with one set of teachers and in another with others.
This inconsistency is likely to lead many pupils to
see the school rules as an arbitrary imposition.
Again, it is likely that all the rules in such a
case may fall into disrepute.

5.2.1 Illustrative Material: Playground Fights.

A primary school, concerned about the amount
of fighting in the playground, asked the School
Support Unit to undertake a project to examine this
aspect of its school rules and their application.
The first step was to broaden the discussion of this
issue to all the adults who took duties in the playground. This involved one discussion with teachers,
and a subsequent one with ancillary staff. Although
both groups acknowledged that the fighting in the
playground constituted a difficulty, there were differences both about what was perceived as a serious
fight, and about how fights were dealt with. The
difficulty was to bring about some discussion between these two groups, so that a clearer and more cohesive policy could be developed concerning what
constituted a breach of the no-fighting-in-the-play-
ground rule and how to deal with any breaches.

Both groups agreed to complete a simple observation schedule to categorise different types of
playground fighting, and the consequent actions
taken. This schedule was completed by the teachers
and the ancillaries on duty each break and lunchtime for two weeks. The idea was to try to gain a
more precise record of the type and frequency of
fights, and to focus attention on the consequence
of actions taken by adults. It is important to note
that the schedule was drawn up after the discussions
with the staff groups, and that the actual paperwork

and organisation of the recording was done by the
school. Needless to say, there were some misunder-
standings and omissions in the recording, but these
were handled with good humour by the head teacher
and, in fact, provoked further dialogue about the
nature of the recording exercise.

At the end of the two week recording period a
member of the Support Unit assisted the school in
analysing and tabulating the responses. The two main
results were: firstly, that there were not as many
fights as either teachers or helpers had thought
there would be; secondly, that the different groups
viewed the incidents differently. Teachers thought
that more of the incidents were serious than did the
ancillary staff. Teachers tended to deal with incidents themselves, whereas the helpers tended to want
to send the pupil(s) to the head teacher. The dis-
tribution of the results among all participants
caused much talk, not only within groups, but also
across groups, even before a formal discussion was
held. The discussion meeting resulted in no firm
decision for action. However, the 'objectivity' of
the results allowed views to be expressed by staff
which might not have been possible without the project framework, and the knowledge that outsiders were
present to give, as it were, permission for people
to state their opinions. The teachers expressed the
view that they would like the helpers to deal with
fights themselves rather than send the protagonists
inside to the head teacher. The helpers thought that
the teachers should ignore many fights but deal more
strictly and firmly with the serious ones.

It seemed at the time that, because no decisions
were taken about changes of practice, the project
was left somewhat in the air. But, a few weeks later,
the head teacher remarked that fewer pupils were
being sent for playground fighting, and that the
staff felt that the difficulty had not been as serious as they had first thought.

On reflection, it seemed that a framework of
expectations had been set by the organisation of the
school in terms of the staffing of the playground
and the lack of formal opportunities for the teacher
group and the helper group to communicate openly
with one another. Within this framework, anxiety
was generated about playground fighting which, in
turn, caused a mis-perception of the frequency of
the incidents. The project opened channels of communication and allowed a reframing of the difficulty
in such a way that all the staff felt confident
enough to deal with fights themselves without so

139

much help from the head teacher, or, indeed, from outside the school.

5.2.2 Illustrative Material: Secondary School Staff Agreement on Rules.

A secondary school was concerned about the general restlessness that it noticed in its second year classes. After several discussions between the two support teachers and both senior staff and subject teachers, it was agreed that the support teachers should spend one week observing as many second year classes as possible. They drew up a schedule and agreed with the school teachers to look at pupils' preparations for tasks at various points of the lesson including the entering and leaving of classes. The observations, then, recorded frequencies of such pupil behaviours as having the correct books, having correct equipment, listening to instructions, movement around the class, readiness to enter and leave classrooms. The school teachers insisted that the support teachers should report their findings exactly as the schedules showed, warts and all.

When the results were fed back, it was the entering and leaving classrooms that provided the topic of most common interest between teachers. In discussion they discovered that they all had slightly different rules about entering classrooms. Some insisted on the pupils lining up, some on silence, others on waiting for the teacher to enter first. They could not all agree on all three of these rules, some teachers observing that their lessons did not require such regimentation or conformity. However, they did agree that they would tell the second year that all classes would be expected to line up outside the classroom before each lesson. The corollary to this was that the teachers themselves had to give top priority to being at or in their classrooms at the beginning of each lesson. The implementation of this rule systematically did indeed lead to a reduction in the level of perceived restlessness and noise.

Given the premise that all pupil behaviour must be considered in its context, then it is appropriate to work not only with individual pupils but also directly with groups of teachers on the context itself. In many cases the context consists of one of the aspects of school organisation.

5.3 Timetabling.

If there is one activity in secondary school which gives the head or deputy an ulcer even before the start of Autumn term, it is the construction of the timetable. It is also one of the processes least open to consultation or democratic control. Yet the division of time affects every aspect of the organisation of the school. Very few secondary schools have yet managed to dispense with the bell or buzzer which forms a lasting memory from which ex-pupils must struggle to liberate themselves. Work habits that last a lifetime are classically conditioned to bells and buzzers.

Yet in primary schools this method of dividing time is becoming rare. Primary schools have pre-set breaks and lunchtimes, but most class teachers decide what activities should occur in their classrooms, most rely on their own timekeeping to bring class periods to an end, some allow children to remain in classrooms during break time to finish work. Some primary schools even give their pupils a degree of responsibility in arranging their daily or weekly timetables. This freedom is not possible in secondary schools where pupils need to make regular contact with a range of specialist teachers and facilities.

There are at least three important implications of timetabling for pupil behaviour. Firstly, timetabling assumes that each pupil has a certain level of personal organisation in order to be at the right place at the right time with the right materials. Not all pupils are initially as organised as this, and some may need to be taught how to comply effectively with the exigencies of the timetable. Others may quickly learn that being disorganised has more pay-offs in terms of attention from teachers and peer group than struggling with timetable constraints. There are many opportunities that arise from being late, in the wrong place or without the right materials.

Secondly, timetabling generally leads to children moving around in groups. For ease of organisation these groups usually remain the same from subject to subject and can conveniently be registered as tutor groups. Tutor groups are usually the main unit of pastoral care in secondary schools. A trend has emerged for setting tutor group time aside on the timetable. This seems to set apart the development of social and personal skills as almost another teaching specialism. The effects of this move towards specialisation on pupil behaviour are yet to be assessed.

Thirdly, as a result of timetabling certain subjects regularly precede and follow others. Pupils
and teachers alike have difficulty in switching attention and motivation on and off to the sound of
bells. The atmosphere of one lesson - be it purposeful or chaotic - is, then, likely to spill over into
the next. A necessary skill for teachers is to be
able to reduce the disruptive carry-over from one
lesson to the next. Carry-over is especially likely
if the composition of the group remains the same from
lesson to lesson, as it does with mixed ability
groups.

From the pupils' point of view, the day can still
be perceived as a whole, despite timetabling, with
teachers joining them at regular intervals to 'sell'
their subjects. However, the unifying and pre-eminent
theme of each day may well be the social transactions
within the group. From the teachers' point of view,
the day is a series of staccato exchanges with different groups, each of which is a small part in the
long process of education. They have to believe that
aims will be achieved in the long term in order to
be able to withstand short-term set-backs.

Outside intervention is unlikely to be able to
affect the timetabling - as distinct from the curriculum - of a secondary school. However, Support Unit
interventions have sometimes touched on this element.
When, after discussion, a pupil asks to be transferred from a tutor group into which he or she does
not seem to fit, the change in group effectively
means a change in timetable. One pupil who did this
remarked later that things were improved not because
he was getting on better with other pupils in the
group, but because his new timetable meant that each
day had at least one of his favourite lessons as an
incentive, whereas prev…siouly two days of the week
had had no bright spots.

5.3.1 <u>Illustrative Material: Organising Time in a
Primary Classroom.</u> The primary day is usually
divided into four long time periods which are then
split into quite short periods by the switching of
activities. With careful planning of groups and resources it is possible for teachers to make activities follow one another so that one acts as a reinforcement for the other.

An eight-year-old boy was referred to the Support Unit because he was frequently shouting out to
get the teacher's attention. When this behaviour was
observed in the classroom, it was noted that it always occurred when the children were meant to be

writing, and usually soon after the teacher had given instructions about the task. The pupil's inter-
jection was often of the nature, "Miss, what do I
do?" At this, the teacher could become annoyed with
replies like, "Haven't you been listening?" or "For
heaven's sake, I've just told you." Subsequent analysis ruled out the possibilities that the boy did
not understand the work, or that he had poor listening skills. It seemed that, perhaps, the behaviour
was reinforced by the teacher's attention. Further
observation showed that these were the only occasions
on which the boy received individual attention from
the teacher, apart from when she marked his book.
    The class teacher then had the idea of starting
the day with a practical activity rather than with
writing. This change allowed the teacher time to
circulate around the class and give positive individual attention. The boy was absorbed by most practical tasks, and so was likely to receive the teacher's interest and praise. The writing task was
then set later. After a week of this simple change
in the order of activities, it was observed that the
boy's shouting out had decreased markedly. When he
did shout out, it was more likely to be to say,
"Miss, come and look at this."
    Interestingly, this class teacher, having
achieved success through this small change, went on
quite spontaneously to make other organisational
changes. Within a year, she had moved from being a
class teacher who taught all the class the same thing
at the same time to one who organised different groups
to do different things at the same time. She organised the class into four groups with different activities such that two were always absorbing and easy
to explain without too much teacher attention, and
two were more complex and needed teacher help and
support. Most of the time, then, she was only talking to about a quarter of the class. She could then
advise them specifically, personally, and without
needing to raise her voice. The classroom developed
a quiet and purposeful atmosphere.

5.4 Teacher Responsibilities.

Running a school is essentially a co-operative
exercise in which members of staff have tasks which
fit together and depend on each other. However, since
the tasks are mutually dependent, it is not always
easy to define the responsibilities so exactly that
they are fixed and fully understood by all concerned.
In fact, responsibilities within a school are often
continually shifting. Unfortunately, with regard to

disruptive behaviour, it is usually necessary to have
clear lines of responsibility which are commonly understood and accepted.

In primary schools, the class teacher is responsible for a group of pupils, and the head and deputy have relationships with individual pupils and
their parents which can assist the class teacher.
When pupils engage in disruptive behaviour, it is
that key relationship with the class teacher which
needs to be supported. The question then arises as
to whether the class teacher can or wants to share
the responsibility. Sometimes, if the head or deputy
tries to share the responsibility with the class
teacher, the pupil may play one off against the
other and conflicts and jealousies can arise. Outsiders, such as support teachers, coming in to help
with disruptive behaviour, could make the pattern of
responsibility even more complicated. They need to
share responsibilities with the head or deputy and
the class teacher only to give them back in the right
proportions. The task of the outsider, then, is
often to help teachers in primary schools share their
responsibilities effectively.

The organisation of secondary schools is usually
very different. The pupils may meet up to eight different teachers in one day. The question, when disruptive behaviour occurs, is who, amidst the variety
of teachers, is going to take responsibility for
doing something about it? If any one teacher steps
forward as a likely candidate for the job, other teachers will all too eagerly relinquish it to him or
her. In some schools, the responsibility can shift
alarmingly quickly from a form tutor, to a year head,
to a deputy head, to a head teacher, to an outside
support person. One of the main tasks of pastoral
systems is to have a recognised chain of responsibility for doing something about disruptive behaviour.
The task of an outsider, such as a support teacher,
is to strengthen and clarify the chains of responsibility within a school rather than in any way seeking to replace them.

Interventions by the Support Unit invariably
must address this issue of responsibility. Usually,
the vehicle for locating and clarifying responsibilities has been the referral of an individual pupil.
Occasionally, however, a school has expressly asked
the team to help them examine the pattern of responsibilities, as in the illustrative material (5.4.1)
overleaf.

5.4.1 <u>Illustrative Material: Changing Pastoral Responsibilities in a Secondary School.</u> A secondary head teacher was concerned that the pastoral
and discipline responsibilities of the school were
being taken on too much by the two deputy heads
rather than by the heads of year and subject teachers.
She saw this as largely due to historical factors as
the two deputies had been at the school longer than
most of the other teachers. The head had talked this
over with the deputies,and they had had a staff
meeting to discuss roles and responsibilities. At
this, it had been agreed that subject teachers who
had difficulty with an individual pupil should first
confer with the head of department and ensure the
appropriateness of the curriculum and teaching methods. Only if difficulties persisted should form
tutors be approached: these would then confer with
the head of year. The deputy heads were only to be
involved in emergencies. Despite this agreement,
subject teachers continued to go directly to deputy
heads. The deputies reinforced this short circuit
by seeing the pupil concerned.

The head discussed this situation with the two
support teachers in the school.They,in turn, consulted their colleagues within the team and learnt of a
system in another school which was called a liaison
meeting. This involved one of the deputy heads chairing a regular meeting of heads of year, support
teachers, educational psychologist, head of special
needs and any form tutors who wanted to discuss pupils about whom they were concerned. The support
teachers informed the head about this, and she, in
turn, suggested it at the next meeting with the deputy heads. After appropriate consultation with
other teachers and the educational psychologist, the
system was initiated.

In order to sharpen role definitions, one of
the deputy heads was selected to chair. At first,
the form tutors' descriptions of pupils and their behaviour tended to be over-shadowed by the accounts
of the heads of year and the deputy head. It seemed
that the presence of the form tutors put the heads
of year in a difficult position. The support teachers
attempted to strengthen the status of the heads of
year within the meetings. The meetings were also made
more formal by asking for accounts of pupils to be
submitted in writing in advance. This gave a task to
the form tutors, but made their presence at the
meetings rather redundant, since their information
was already available on paper. It also made the
deputy's task in chairing much simpler and this,

unexpectedly, meant that he himself made a briefer
account of the pupil concerned. The floor was left
more open to the heads of year. After two terms, the
frequency of the liaison meetings was reduced from
once a fortnight to once a month. Meanwhile each head
of year introduced weekly meetings held on a more
formal basis (notes were taken) with his or her own
form tutors. Following this, the form tutors ceased
to come to the liaison meetings, since they were receiving support at their meetings with their respective heads of year. Since these meetings were also
opportunities to prepare accounts of pupils for the
liaison meetings, they still retained a direct chan-
nel of communication.

It is almost impossible to assess the effects
of such an organisational intervention on the behaviour of specific pupils. Perhaps such direct effects were not to be expected. However, the patterns
of responsibility and the ways in which these were
communicated, have both become much clearer and more
effective. At the very least, teacher time was being
used more effectively by the elimination of unclear
and overlapping responsibilities. At best, teachers
became more aware of the nature and limits of their
responsibilities and, thus, more able to fulfill them
without duplicating the efforts of others.

5.5 Communication.

The issue of responsibility may be said to involve who needs to speak to whom, and what about.
Communication, more plainly, involves how successfully information is passed from one person to another. Communications about disruptive behaviour tend
to be some of the most important in a school. Unlike
issues of, say, academic performance, information
may need to be transmitted speedily and to a variety
of people. It is much more likely that feelings -
of teachers, parents, and pupils - will be running
high on this issue, so communications may be constrained, stilted, tense, or angry. Often, the baldness of a statement conceals the emotion with which
it is made, or what is said seems at odds with the
way it is said. Sometimes, communication simply
does not take place, and someone who should be informed of an event in school is not. Information
needs to flow between classroom teachers and those
with management responsibilities, as well as between
those inside the school and those services outside.

Difficulties in this area are not hard to identify. Messages go astray, telephone calls remain

unanswered. Red lights outside head teachers' offices forbid entry to harassed teachers in their one free half-hour in the day. Management staff and outside agencies request time-consuming assessment material from teachers without explaining its purpose, and often without paying much apparent attention to it when it is completed. Teachers fear that communicating difficulties to senior staff may detrimentally affect their career advancement.

Communication includes both formal channels like records or reports, and informal conversations in the corridor, at breaktime or at meetings. Both formal and informal methods need to operate simultaneously. A formal system has the advantage of allowing the writer space for reflection, and of providing a record to which reference can be made. The disadvantages are that writing is time-consuming and may give the writer a false sense of passing on responsibility with the piece of paper. Informal methods have the advantage that the receiver is on the spot to clarify the information or to ask clarifying supplementary questions. Both methods are capable of abuse. Written notes can be used to speed a process up (by exaggerating the seriousness of events or by sending copies higher up a line of management) or to slow it down (knowing that paper moves through certain desks more slowly than through others). Spoken exchanges can lapse into loose talk that commits neither party to any action. Loose teacher talk is one of the mechanisms whereby specific pupils become labelled as disruptive.

Often, even when working on a specific case, Support Unit teachers need to energise communication systems in a school. This can be done by interposing in the communication systems, and giving feedback to all parties. This feedback may begin on an individual basis, but subsequently team teachers may feedback to different parties simultaneously as, for example, in review meetings that may involve two or three teachers, the parent and the pupil. When written communication between teachers in a school is unsystematic or irregular, a team teacher may introduce an element of formality through the referral, assessment and review forms devised by the team (see the Illustrative Material in Chapter 3).

5.5.1 <u>Illustrative Material: A Team Teacher's Misjudgement of a Communication System.</u> The following case uses the diagrammatic form of communication analysis used in Chapter 3. Although the case did not work out as well as the team teacher might have hoped, it did point to ways in which communications in the school could be improved.

A second year girl in a mixed comprehensive school had, prior to referral, developed a manner which was loud and noisy in most lessons. In particular, teachers were reprimanding her for talking back to their instructions in a loud, challenging way. Teachers seemed to see no positive aspects to her behaviour. Eventually the head of year made an appointment with the girl's mother, and pointed out to her the girl's strengths and weaknesses as she saw them. However, it seems that only the negative comments were passed on to the daughter. The girl's behaviour in school continued as before. The teachers actually thought that it deteriorated, but this may have been because, after the interview with the mother, they had expected an improvement. The mother's annoyance with the girl appeared to have had no deterrent effect, and may even have been rewarding for the girl, in that she may have derived some satisfaction in thinking that her mother was in trouble with school. The head of year was also frustrated by the girl's lack of improvement and so became aware more directly and personally of her negative behaviour. Figure 5.1 shows the communication pattern at the time of referral.

Figure 5.1: <u>Communications at the outset</u>

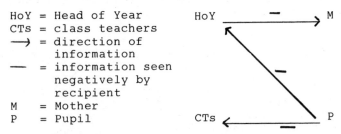

HoY = Head of Year
CTs = class teachers
⟶ = direction of
      information
— = information seen
      negatively by
      recipient
M = Mother
P = Pupil

A negative cycle had been established and a reputation earned. The school had a well used system of written communication for teachers to circulate information about pupils. Negative comments about the girl continued to circulate and so were readily available to be transferred onto the team teacher's referral and assessment forms. The team teacher observed some lessons and saw the girl regularly. So, the team teacher became aware of some of the positive aspects of the girl's school life - some close friendships, a talent for drama and imaginative written work - as well as agreeing fully with the negative aspects which had been perceived by teachers. She started feeding back both the positive and negative aspects to the girl and to the teachers. The teachers adjusted their perception of the girl slightly, and she herself seemed motivated to change.

Whilst this communication was proceeding informally, the head teacher held a regular, formal, half-termly review with all the heads of year about pupils causing difficulties. For this formal meeting the head teacher requested views in writing. The last reports on the girl which the head of year could provide were negative. The head teacher, who knew the girl from having taught her the previous year, decided to see the girl's mother. After this meeting the head instituted a special head teacher's report system on the girl for two weeks. The replies which came back were much more positive and the girl maintained the change, which had actually begun before the head's intervention, with a few temporary lapses.

The teachers in the school naturally attributed the change exclusively to the head teacher's intervention and the credibility of the team teacher suffered. A communication analysis shows that the team teacher had paid too little attention to the influence of the formal communications with the head teacher by the heads of year. She had relied instead on her informal communications with the teachers to filter through to the head of year. Figure 5.2. shows this analysis after the team teacher had been working for six weeks.

Figure 5.2: <u>Communications after six weeks.</u>

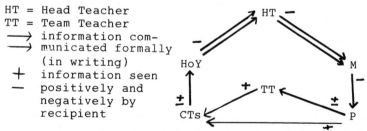

HT = Head Teacher
TT = Team Teacher
⟶ information communicated formally (in writing)
+ information seen positively and
− negatively by recipient

The team teacher had energised the informal communications between the pupil and the teachers and made them more open. She had failed to appreciate the significance of the formal communication system in the school.

Of course, as far as the case was concerned, the important thing was the improvement in the girl's behaviour, irrespective of who was credited with bringing it about. The team teacher realised, however, that she needed to be more firmly integrated in the school's formal communication system. She made a suggestion to the head, jointly with the head of year with whom she had been working on this case, that she should be able to make contributions to the half-termly formal reviews. This was agreed and initially led to her giving any relevant views to the heads of year before the meetings. After two terms, the team teacher additionally submitted her own regular reports. After three terms, the team teacher assisted the heads of year in redesigning the report form, that class teachers used to contribute to the formal review, in order to make it more specific in the descriptions of behaviour it elicited.

5.6 Contact with parents.

The contacts that schools make with parents vary markedly both according to the type of school (infant, junior, secondary) and also between schools of the same type. Recent documents such as the "Hargreaves Report" (Hargreaves, D.H. et al., 1984) have reflected a trend to place increasing emphasis on the positive part that parents can play in the life of the school as governors, as classroom helpers, as students themselves, and as a source of support and encouragement to their own children. The 1980 and 1981 Education Acts have given parents the crucial role in the selection of schools and in the consultation process concerning their children's future educational opportunities. Some schools have, in consequence, radically reviewed the nature of their contact with parents. Yet, with regard to disruptive behaviour, schools' contacts with parents often remain negative. Parents are sent letters complaining of their children's misdemeanours or are summoned to school for a more direct rebuke. Few letters contain good news, and improvements in behaviour or performance are often left without comment. Yet, pupils when asked what would be a reward for appropriate behaviour may choose a letter home.

The model of classroom disruption adopted by the Schools Support Unit placed the phenomenon firmly in the classroom and the school. Attempts to locate the difficulty as stemming from the pupil's family or home life were resisted. The team emphasised changing school practices, which are under the control of teachers, rather than trying to change parent practices which are not. There was, however, some work with parents on individual cases, which was described in the previous chapter. When team teachers talk to parents it is about what happens, or is intended to happen, in school.They are trying to encourage the parents' active support for the pupil in school. This may be necessary either because the parents lack interest in school, or because the relationship with the school has broken down and the team teacher is endeavouring to re-build bridges. The team teacher's work with the parents is largely a matter of making the school more accessible to them. A central objective, therefore, is to bring them into closer communication with teachers in school, and to start (or re-start) a dialogue about the needs of the child, and what they can jointly do to meet them. The team's contact with parents had led to the running of groups for parents (nine up to the time of writing). These have involved groups of parents from different schools, and groups of parents from the same school. The groups have either focused on behaviour management or problems of communication with teachers.

5.6.1 Illustrative Material: A Group for Parents.
    Mutual problem-solving groups for parents, whose children have been getting into trouble in schools, have been established in both primary and secondary schools. Most of the organisation of the groups, in terms of inviting parents and providing accommodation and equipment was done by the schools. The sessions were run by two members of the support team, a teacher and the education welfare officer. As a result of evaluating one series of sessions, it was discovered that, once parents had developed confidence in the group leaders and familiarity with the school, they wanted to work more intensively on behaviour problems than was possible in the weekly sessions. A further group was, therefore, arranged consisting of five daily sessions in one week. The results were encouraging. Parents presented much more pressing problems and were able to discuss solutions which they could try out over the next few days. The immediacy of the feedback and the close support that the group generated produced some substantial practical changes for some parents. The focus was on day to day behaviour difficulties.

Parents were prepared to experiment by, making changes in their own responses to difficult behaviour at home and, if necessary, in their household routines.

Groups such as this are labour-intensive, but they may have a preventative long-term effect. However, some evidence to this effect would need to be forthcoming before resources could be committed to them on a large scale.

5.7 In-service training and in-school support.

A great deal of valuable in-service training is organised across schools by local authorities, polytechnics, and university departments of education. This puts teachers in touch with current developments and pratices, and adds to their knowledge and skills. Such work, however, is rarely either school-focused or school-based. It is a very different sort of training and support which is required if the knowlege and skills are going to be put effectively into practice, because changes need to take place in the organisation of a school to facilitate such innovation. These changes may be in curriculum, timetabling, or responsibilities, but they also involve changes in attitude and constant support from members of staff at each different level. Two levels of in-service training may perhaps be distinguished: the first, general and informative; the second, school-based, school-focused, and directly concerned with changes in practice.

The Schools Support Unit has been active at both these levels in providing training in how to prevent and deal with disruptive behaviour in schools. At the general level, members of the team have run sessions for probationary teachers, spoken on general courses at teachers centres, and given sessions for groups of head teachers and educational psychologists. Team teachers have similarly contributed in a general way to schemes of in-service training organised by the schools in which they are working.

At the school-based, school-focused level, whenever the team has been involved, it has been concerned to build in support in school for subsequent changes in teacher practice. This applies to both the systematic courses offered by the Unit (see Illustrative Material 5.2.7 below) and to courses run by individual team members for groups of teachers in a specific school. This support has been achieved in two ways. Firstly, the nature of the training has been discussed in advance with the head of any participating school and as many of his or her ideas as possible incorporated in it. Even if the head takes no further part in the process, and it is to be hoped that he or she will, his or her positive support is imperative. Secondly, training is only offered when a group of teachers from the same school can attend, or when the whole group is exclusively from one school. By working with several members of staff from the same school, it is possible during a course to discuss what changes in practice might be needed, and how these could be implemented. The implementation requires consultation with relevant members of staff, including those not involved in the training, in order to proceed with a consensus of approval. It also requires the arrangement of some support sessions in school time, outside the timetable of the course. The sessions can assist teachers by noticing when changes are developing well, and by encouraging consistency of practice and persistence when things go wrong, as they sometimes do. If in-service training in the area of preventing classroom disruption is to be effective, it is probably essential that those offering the course should spend some time in the school and classroom with the teachers taking the course. Only in this way can changes in practice be encouraged and support within the school organisation mobilised. With several teachers from one school involved in a course, mutual support and encouragement is also likely to help to develop change.

5.7.1 Illustrative Material: Courses for Teachers in School.
This is an account of two large-scale courses run by team members for teachers in primary schools. In both cases, the courses were evaluated by asking the participants to fill in a questionnaire at the end of the final session. The questionnaire asked what they had found useful, whether the mode of presentation was appropriate to the subject, what were the main omissions, and how the course could be improved. The evaluation of the first course provided a basis on which to adjust the second; the evaluation of the second provided a basis on which further courses could be planned.

The courses were intended to meet two of the aims of the Unit: to develop teachers' skills in dealing with classroom disruption; to develop school organisations in which disruption is likely to be minimised. The latter aim was a major consideration in planning the second course, which was offered to the entire staffs of three schools.

Both courses followed a workshop model. Each weekly session was introduced by a short talk from a member of the Unit to the entire group. The meeting then split up into small groups, each with a leader from the Unit. These groups not only discussed the topic, but also organised follow-up work which the teachers could do in their schools. If the session was a classroom observation, for instance, schedules were worked out which the teachers felt happy about using for a specific child or group of children in their own class. The team members attempted to visit participants from their small group in their classrooms later in the week in order to help with the follow-up work. This class contact in - between sessions enlivened the small group session the following week. The first course consisted of eight sessions in one term: the first dealt with behaviour-specific description; the next two with classroom observation; sessions four and five were on classroom management; then followed two sessions on behaviour management with individual children; the final session was for feedback and observation.

The results of the evaluation were encouraging. The usefulness of the behaviour-specific description, classroom management techniques and behaviour management were particularly stressed. The mode of presentation was favourably regarded, especially the chance to talk in small, familiar groups. The main improvement which the teachers suggested was to run the course in any other term than the busy one which precedes the summer holidays.

The evaluation seemed to indicate that little change was needed in planning the next course except in the timing. Nevertheless, the team members involved felt that the course could be more effective if it were more school-based and school-focused. It was hoped that this would lead to improvements in school organisation as well as developing teacher skills. Three schools were approached, and all decided that they would like to participate with all their staff. They were a large JM and I, and separate infant and junior schools which shared a common site. Significantly, the issue of whether or not to participate was decided in the JM and I school at a staff meeting attended by the course co-ordinator. In the other schools, the heads consulted informally and then responded themselves.

Four team members ran the sessions as the group of thirtyfour teachers was split up into only three workshops, one for each school. The JM and I staff had two team members in their rather large workshop.

This was in conflict with the evaluation finding that teachers enjoyed the opportunity to discuss in small groups, but it was felt necessary to keep the school staffs together if school organisation aspects were to be discussed. The same format of short talk, discussion, workshop and follow-up in school was followed. There were eight sessions:the first was on behaviour-specific description; the second on observation techniques, the next two were on classroom management, followed by two on strategies of individual children; there was then a session on whole school strategies; the final session included a discussion of the support services available in the area as well as devoting time to evaluation.

The results of the evaluation questionnaire (which had the high reply rate of 29 out of 34) were less unambiguous than after the first course. Whilst most teachers approved of the material and mode of presentation, a few (4) thought the small groups lacked leadership or that participation by teachers was a significant omission (6). Many (10) wanted smaller groups and a few (7 in each case) would have liked shorter introductory talks with more case material. There were obvious differences between the responses of the various schools: all six of the replies which used the word 'excellent' were from teachers in the JM and I school; all the six who would have preferred to have participated without the other schools came from the infant school.

After considering the responses to the questionnaires, the course co-ordinator drew the following conclusions:-

1. A less ambitious course for one school, involving only two Unit staff might now seem to be advisable;
2. Keeping introductory talks down to twenty minutes is essential;
3. The support services session could be completely cut, and the observation session needs to be merged with one other;
4. Preliminary discussion with staff as well as heads seems essential;
5. Group discussion leaders need to adopt an overtly directive approach and to achieve participation in the first session.

These comments were perhaps unduly gloomy. The two courses certainly met their aims to some extent. The following four quotations are reasonably typical: they are taken from responses from teachers on the second course concerning what elements in it they

found useful.
"Created awareness for need for greater discussion
in school among teachers." "It's made me think of my
own classroom attitude and manner, and how it has
affected (sic) my class." "After discussing the effect of changing the classroom around upon the children, I had a grand re-shuffle in mine - it was a
great success with the class - they like the new
arrangements very much." "Whole school strategies -
very important, and this is where we needed someone
to get us thinking constructively." On the other hand,
this is a reply to what were the main omissions on
the second course: "Not starting from where we were
in our schools and not accounting for our own experience and interests." Two other respondents answered in a similar vein.

Although it may be concluded that this method
of work is effective, three reservations may be
noted. Firstly, both these courses were with primary
teachers, and modifications would have been needed to
work in a comprehensive school. Secondly, it is
essential to have commitment from the participating
teachers at the outset. When a whole school course
is planned, this necessitates consultation with all
the staff before the commencement of the course.
Thirdly, this method of working demands a large
commitment of time from members of the team. The
people running the courses as well as those taking
them had had a hard day in school before they
started.

5.8 Intervening in School Organisations.

Work with individual pupils and teachers actually goes hand in hand with work with the school as
an organisation. Whatever the context of the work,
people intervening in such complex institutions as
schools need to proceed with extreme caution. The
following five rules are offered not to indicate a
mode of procedure, but rather to try to pre-empt
some of the most serious blunders:

1. Always work through the head teacher in the first
   place.
2. Clarify in advance the nature and length of the
   commitment being made.
3. Do not underestimate how long it takes to become
   accepted.
4. Concentrate on feeding back observations and providing structures for insiders to make observations, so that they can gain insight into the

workings of their own organisation.
5. Do not plan change for people in the school,
    but ensure that they find support for the chan-
    ges that they plan.

Intervening in schools raises questions concerning the organisation of support and advisory
staff. These questions are the subject of the next
chapter.

Chapter 6

THE ROLE AND FUNCTION OF SUPPORT SERVICES IN A LOCAL EDUCATION AUTHORITY

6.1 Support services and the 1981 Education Act.

This chapter widens the perspective of the pre-ceding argument which showed how a support team can successfully reduce disruption in mainstream schools. It examines the implications of the organisation of this type of support service for the education of all children perceived to have special needs or handi-caps. It considers whether such a service is best arranged as an outside peripatetic team, or as a school-based provision, or a mixture of both. It also looks at the necessary organisational and management structures and how such changes may be planned.

The 1981 Education Act was implemented in 1983 after some delay. Despite hope on many sides, not the least parents, that this would rapidly ease the inte-gration of children perceived to have special educa-tional needs into ordinary schools, the progress has been hesitant. The Act gave LEA's three obvious 'get-out' clauses, allowing them to treat the idea of in-tegration in whatever way suited them best. Integra-tion was not deemed to be appropriate, for any given individual pupil, if it were inappropriate to the needs of the child, if it would interfere with the education of children in ordinary schools, or if it were to cost too much. The variety of interpretation of those clauses leaves ample room for all courses of action, including none at all. The working of the Act mirrors the traditional ambivalence about cen-tralised control in the British education system, wavering between, on the one hand, the attraction of the rationality of central control which, by its in-herent fairness, would provide similar services in different parts of the country, and, on the other, respect for the autonomy of LEA's and, within LEA's themselves, for the autonomy of head teachers and

158

school governors.

By contrast, the new full assessment procedures outlined in the Act seemed to be more firmly binding on parents, those professionals concerned with assessment and authorities alike. For the first time, formal procedures were laid down in a legal framework. In many cases, authorities have appointed educational psychologists to draw up the new statements (Gipps C., and Gross H., 1984) whilst retaining, or even continuing to expand, their existing segregated special school and off-site provision. The result is that to the extent that the process of integration is being initiated in England and Wales, it is happening in a patchy, piecemeal manner, largely according to the reforming zeal of authority members, inspectors, and officers.

For this reason, no clear picture of the most suitable organisational models has yet emerged. Accounts of integration schemes have tended to concentrate on individual cases of good practice mostly in particular schools (Heggarty, S., Pockington, K. 1981; 1982; Booth, T. and Potts, P. (Eds.), 1983).

The work of the peripatetic team outlined in preceding chapters may offer a more generalisable model. But is it applicable to the education of children whose special needs are very different from those who are perceived to indulge in disruptive behaviour?

It has usually been pupils with behaviour difficulties who have been seen as the hardest to integrate. The growth in the last two decades in the number of places in special schools for the maladjusted, or in behavioural units (Booth, T., 1981) could be seen as evidence of this in the U.K. If a peripatetic team has achieved some success in supporting these pupils in mainstream school, then similar results may be possible for pupils currently educated in special schools. Special educational needs in the ordinary school in the form of learning problems, sensory or motor problems, or social problems, cannot be separated from the needs of teachers (to develop suitable curriculum and appropriate teaching methods) and the needs of a school as an organisation (to communicate successfully about the performance of pupils both within itself and to people outside, especially parents). Thus working with disruption sometimes means working with underlying special educational needs and always means working with teachers and with schools. This is the main relevance of the team's work to the integration of special needs.

However, if we are considering the integration of pupils with moderate learning difficulties, with

sensory or physical handicaps, a team intervention
approach cannot, on its own, provide a complete procedure. Some (but not all) of such pupils will need
specially adapted classrooms, or specialised equipment,
or specialised teaching, in terms of presentation
and teaching method. Where architectural adaptations
are required, it may be cost effective to group
children needing them in specific mainstream schools.
The idea of designated units in ordinary schools has
been a practice of some authorities for a number of
years. With advances in computer assisted learning
(CAL) and gradual reductions in costs of computer
equipment, then in time it should be less and less
necessary, from a financial and logistical point of
view, to group pupils needing specialised equipment
or teaching methods together. However, there will
still be a need for specialist teachers for such pupils, since the learning difficulties of pupils and
the materials and methods required will remain highly individualised. Not all teachers would be expected
to be proficient in such areas of specialist expertise and experience, but they would need to know
about them, since in a policy of integration many
pupils requiring specialist teaching will be in ordinary classes. Furthermore, the theory and practice
of individualised learning programmes is relevant to
all pupils. The specialist teacher, we believe, has
a great deal to offer the class teacher or subject
teacher and vice versa, but they do need a framework
through which such an exchange of skills and knowledge can take place.

A specialist teacher may see a pupil with special
needs three or more times a week, and may need to
spend as much time working alongside class teachers.
For this reason, the level of collaboration over
curriculum planning would need to be considerable.
Team teachers from the support team described in
earlier chapters may see individual pupils up to three
times a week and spend considerable time with class
teachers, but the amount of time spent on curriculum
matters is small. For this reason, specialist teachers may be better based in schools and yet, working
from a team base, they may be better placed to offer
support (rather than expertise) to the class teacher.

6.2 School-based or team-based specialist support teachers?

Support for children perceived to have special
needs may be school-based or team-based. An examination of the respective advantages might help to

determine which is appropriate in the circumstances of specific LEA's.

6.2.1 <u>Advantages of school-based services.</u> A support teacher based in a school or a group of such teachers in a larger school with professional and administrative responsibility to the head would have the advantage of closer links with other members of staff. They would be unlikely to be regarded with the suspicion and reserve which is often the initial response of teachers to people coming in from outside. This may mean that the organisation of potentially difficult interventions in classrooms such as observation, behaviour programmes, precision teaching or team teaching is facilitated.

A second clear advantage is that school-based support teachers would be committed full time to the school. It would not be necessary for them to divide their attention between schools or to attend team meetings elsewhere. It may be, however, that there are not enough pupils in a primary school to warrant one specialist support teacher. Otherwise, the special needs of the pupils may be rather different and beyond the knowledge and experience of the teacher in the school. There are two solutions to this problem which would be a third advantage in favour of being based in a school. The first is that all school-based support teachers should be specialists in two areas: learning difficulties and behaviour problems. In fact, if behaviour problems were thought of as social learning problems, the teachers could be called genuine learning support teachers. Where pupils presented themselves with other needs (such as partial deafness or poor eyesight), they could call on the services of peripatetic specialists, like the present peripatetic teachers for sensory impaired children, who would have the additional role of training the learning support teacher, so that he or she could withdraw from the school in due course. The second solution is that all school-based support teachers ought not to concentrate all their time and efforts on children perceived to have special needs. If they were to do some mainstream teaching or, in a secondary school, be responsible for teaching their subject for part of the timetable, this would increase their status with other teachers. This might also be to the benefit of the children perceived to have special needs, in that they would not be seen to be the sole responsbility of teachers who were exclusively devoted to them. This arrangement would also mean that all departments of a school would have to adapt themselves to meet special needs, but have support teachers who, as subject teachers in their departments, would bring their own special skills and interest to curriculum development.

A fourth advantage concerns career opportunities. Teachers who are based outside school sometimes find that their experience is regarded with some suspicion when they come to apply for senior posts back in mainstream. However, if such teachers opt to stay out of mainstream and obtain promotion within the career structure of outside support teachers, they might find themselves at an early age stuck at the top of a short career ladder. A school-based support teacher's chances of obtaining a post as head or deputy head would be further enhanced, if they maintained a teaching contact with the majority of children.

A fifth advantage is the fact that support teachers may be likely, with enhanced prospects of promotion within the school, to stay in a school post longer than they would stay in a peripatetic team. This would mean that they could stay in contact with special needs pupils for perhaps the whole of that pupil's stay in the school instead of two or three years for a peripatetic teacher.

The sixth advantage is the major implication which the integration of special needs has for all departments and systems within a school. It will affect pastoral systems and, if it reduces the frequency of behaviour problems which now occur mainly because learning problems are not being met, then pastoral systems will have more time to concentrate on positive pastoral work with individuals and with groups.

Summary of advantages of school-based services:

1. Close links with all members of staff.
2. Full-time commitment to one school.
3. Special needs teachers would also do some mainstream teaching and so be committed to subject departments, thereby sharing skills.
4. Combining mainstream teaching with special needs support would enhance career prospects.
5. Long-term contacts with pupils (4-5 years instead of 2-3 years for teachers in peripatetic teams).
6. Pastoral staff have more time for positive work.

6.2.2 Advantages of Team-based services. A team-based service would carry out many of the teaching and resource functions of special needs teachers now in schools. It would be responsible for

direct teaching services (part of the week) to specially referred and assessed individual pupils and
for co-ordinating with school staffs over resources
and teaching methods for such children in mixed
ability groups (indirect services). In order to do
this, such a team would need to be large (one teacher per 4 primary schools or per 2 secondary schools).
Managing such a team may be easier if it were split
on a geographical basis or, alternatively, split on
an age-range basis. The team would also need to be
multi-disciplinary, with fixed sessions from educational psychologists and educational welfare officers.
This would help to fulfil the assessment functions
of the team. Such personnel would also contribute to
in-service training within the team and to planning
joint in-service between the team and schools.

The first advantage of such a team is the dan-
gerous credibility of outside experts. This is very
much a two-edged weapon. The team would be expected
by school teachers to demonstrate expertise. But
this disposition to trust expertise may well be tem-
pered with a certain degree of suspicion and resentment of outside help. At the same time, the team
would only be fully successful in its work, if it
were able to transfer some of its expertise to teachers in schools, so that they could continue to
exercise their responsibility for pupils with special
needs in their schools. The finesse of achieving
such a transfer of skills (covert in-service training)
is not to be underestimated. The pay-offs for schools
are large, but so are the risks to the credibility
of the team. If the transfer of skills proves too
difficult, all that happens is that the teacher in
school feels de-skilled. For the credibility of outside experts to be an advantage, a team would need
the resources (time and expertise) to be able to provide training and support to its members in managing
it.

The second advantage is more obvious and less
risky. Being based outside a school lends one the
advantage of neutrality. This is perhaps most relevant when pupils with difficulties prove to be the
source of some conflict between adults (teacher and
teacher, teacher and parent). Such conflict is not
unusual over behaviour difficulties, which may even
be maintained by the existence of conflict, and over
learning difficulties, since they will give rise to
failure and frustration. The neutrality of a third
person would be helpful in any case where a child
feels inadequately understood by the teachers or,
indeed, where a teacher is at odds with senior

teachers. A neutral participant may see a situation
from a different perspective, because the school
protagonists are too familiar with it, or because
their feelings colour their judgement too strongly.
A neutral outsider may be able to suggest changes
in class, curriculum or even school, or, better
still, mediate in a conflict so that both parties
find some areas of agreement and can move forward
again.

A third advantage is that the support from a
team can be at various levels within a school at
the same time. Thus, the support may be ostensibly
for a pupil or group of pupils. But, in order to
offer this effectively, a team teacher often has to
support a class teacher or subject teachers or even
senior teachers.

A fourth advantage is that support teachers can
foster links between schools and outside agencies
where personnel from such agencies do not have the
time to visit schools as frequently as they would
wish. This is particularly true, when the team is
multi-disciplinary, having members such as social
workers and psychologists who also belong to other
teams in the area. A support team, to give genuine
learning support to pupils and teachers, may also
have attached part-time some specialist support teachers (e.g. for sensory handicapped) or other professionals (e.g. speech therapists or medical officers) to give their advice over assessment and to
assist in in-service training within the team.

A fifth advantage is the flexibility in a team
teacher's timetable. They can devote more or less
time to a specific school as circumstances change,
or as need arises. This response is likely to be
more adaptive than that of a school which has so
many more vested interests in maintaining the status
quo of staffing levels and staff responsibilities.
In terms of meeting the needs of an area, a team-
based service is likely to be more cost-effective in
this respect than a school-based service. The geographical size of an area may be a factor, since
team teachers may visit two or three schools in one
day. They, therefore, need a car and in a large
area the cost of travelling in money and time may
prove a powerful counterbalance to the benefits to
schools.

A sixth advantage may be in terms of support
and training. Any teacher who works with pupils who
have or give difficulties is in need of training
and constant support. In a team, this can be given
top priority and have appropriate resources (time

and expertise) allocated to it. In a school, this may have to take lower priority in the face of other pressures, or at least its priority would be a constant issue with the head teacher.

A seventh advantage accrues again from the multi-disciplinary basis. A generic support team to cover all special needs would benefit from the cross-fertilisation of different knowledge and experience of teachers (types of special training and experience of a range of special needs) as well as the different professional perspectives of various professions who may be attached such as social worker, speech therapist, psychologist, or school doctor. Of course, such a multi-professional service has implications for the organisation of different professions within an authority. Partly because of separate lines of management and funding, and partly because of the tendency of professionals to prefer to group themselves with people of similar orientation and expertise, many authorities still retain patterns of provision which are separated into watertight compartments. A multi-disciplinary team would have greater access to the services of the various professions, and may lead to greater speed and efficiency in working with joint referrals.

An eighth and final advantage would be that a team would offer an authority-wide perspective and be able to liaise with other authority-wide systems such as administrators and advisers. A team would be able to provide useful statistics on authority-wide trends in the pattern of needs and give advice in planning the allocation of resources not only to the team itself, but to schools or groups of schools. The advantage would not only be at a level of planning. It would also apply to such problems as primary-secondary school liaison, in-service training across schools, and exchange of good practice between schools.

Summary of advantages of team-based services:

1. Credibility of outside expertise.
2. Neutrality in situations of conflict.
3. Support at various levels in a school simultaneously.
4. Liaison between schools and outside agencies.
5. Flexibility of team to meet a school's or an area's need by re-distributing resources.
6. Priority for support and training for special needs teachers.

7. Cross-fertilisation of skills in a multi-disciplinary team.
8. Authority-wide perspective for exchange of good practice between schools, primary - secondary liaison, and planning in-service training.

6.3 The organisation and control of support services.

How the relative advantages of team-based or school-based services weigh will clearly depend on what services already exist in an area, what sort of climate for change exists in the various administrative and professional systems that would be affected, and the nature of the organisation and control of support services. It is this latter question which will now be examined.

But, firstly, it is necessary to understand why organisation and control are important. If schools felt that they had some control over a team-based service, they may be more inclined to see its advantages. Equally, if advisers and administrators felt that they had some control over school-based services, they may be more inclined to see their advantages.

The issue of organisation and control is important because it has to do with the spending of large amounts of public money. Therefore, central to any system of organisation and control must be the twin pillars of accountability (public and professional) and evaluation. By considering the practicality of these concepts more closely, it may be easier to see whether to opt for school-based or team-based services, or a cominbation of the two.

6.3.1 Organisation and control of school-based services. A school-based support service would not be the same as a special needs department in a secondary school, just as the latter is not the same as the former remedial departments. Can such a service actually deal with the whole range of special needs? Is it going to be able to help children with learning difficulties, reduce severe classroom disruption, and produce resources in specific subject areas for e.g. a visually impaired child? Is the service going to be a string of specialists, or are there curriculum teaching methods common to the effective teaching of different children? Perhaps, the most unifying factor between isolated specialists, however, will be the need to be able to work alongside, train and support class and subject teachers. That is what is new about support teaching.

The role and function of support services

It is a hybrid between a direct specialist teaching service and an advisory teacher service. The support teacher has the credibility of a direct teacher and the expertise of an advisor. The range of skills will involve training a teacher who has little or no knowledge in the specialist area by some introduction to theory and by modelling good practice. The skills will also involve helping a teacher to have the confidence and creativity to work out solutions to teaching problems himself or herself, when the knowledge and experience is already there or almost there.

The leader of a school-based service would, therefore, have to be able to train and support his or her teachers in the skills of support teaching as well as organise in-service training to formalise and expedite the sharing of skills between specialists. This task in a primary school would be different from a secondary school because of numbers. The number of teachers available for special needs would depend on what re-allocation of teachers was possible or desirable from those currently working in special schools, off-site centres, or peripatetically. Even if the number of special needs posts were doubled, primary schools may be lucky to have one entire post. That would inevitably mean that the organisation and control of their time would be closely tied to the head or deputy head of the school. As mentioned above, a head might sometimes find it difficult to resist using special needs support time to cover other areas of priority, such as covering for sick teachers, teaching a 'difficult' class, or seeing parents. Perhaps some check or balance on this may be achieved by making a special needs teacher professionally accountable both to the head and to some authority-wide head of special needs.

In a secondary school, the situation is more complicated. With the school's teachers being divided into subject departments, there is a temptation not present in primary school for no single teacher to take responsibility for a pupil's teaching. The theoretical sharing of responsibility between subject teachers can prove too difficult to achieve in practice. The advent of a special needs department may simply serve to allow subject teachers to absolve their responsibility for children with special needs onto the special needs department. That is the danger of forming special needs into another department. If special needs teachers also all had a commitment to mainstream subject teaching, they would naturally have a subject department of which to be a member. They would need to have links with the other special needs teachers, but this could be purely for in-service training and support purposes. The actual administration of providing for special needs pupils would fall on heads of subject departments, with a co-ordinating role given to a deputy head. If co-ordination were in the hands of a deputy head, the same danger would apply as in primary schools - namely that special needs teaching time may be given a lower priority at times of crisis. Therefore, again a special needs teacher may need to have some clear professional accountability towards an authority-wide head of special needs as well as to one of the school's deputy heads.

The notion of an authority-wide head of Special Education may also have some attraction in solving another problem. Inevitably, a secondary school and, even more so, a primary school will occasionally have pupils whose special needs are so unusual that no teacher or teachers in that school have the experience or time to meet them. Therefore, some sort of specialist peripatetic assessment, teaching and support would be needed. Indeed, such pupils may well become the subjects of full assessment statements, if only to secure the authority's commitment to providing appropriate specialist teaching for that pupil over a number of years. These peripatetic specialist teachers may best be formed into a Special Education team, so that their time in schools can be allocated optimally, so that they can support one another, and so that they can liaise formally with educational psychologists for sharing the assessment task and planning interventions and more general in-service training. Such a team would need a leader.

Turning to the management of school-based services, each service would clearly be accountable to the management of each school as a whole. As a matter of good practice, it is suggested that each school carries out periodic evaluations of the organisation and effectiveness of its special needs teaching, in conjunction with evaluations of other aspects of its teaching. For this purpose, a school may well benefit from turning to outsiders for help in planning and carrying out such evaluation. The obvious persons to fulfil this function for special needs are the educational psychologists, the head of the special education team (if such a post were created), and the special education adviser. This role would need to be precisely described for such persons and suitable time allowed for it amid their other duties.

6.3.2 <u>Organisation and control of team-based</u>
<u>services.</u> A prime consideration for a team is
to have a good base with good resources in terms of
staff rooms, telephones, work preparation rooms,
interview rooms, administrative staff and resources
(including media resources officer and micro-
computers). With a good base and careful leadership,
a team of teachers and professionals, even from
different theoretical backgrounds and with disparate
experience, can be forged into a coherent team.
     The lines of responsibility within a team would
be complicated but not unworkable. Since the team
is likely to consist largely of teachers, then it is
sensible for a teacher to be in charge. A team of
15-20 may merit a senior teacher scale for the
teacher-in-charge. If 2 or 3 teams of that number
were required, split according to age-ranges of pupils, then a head teacher scale would be more appropriate. It would be inappropriate, however, for a
teacher-in-charge to take responsibility for the work
of other professionals attached to the team. Social
workers or psychologists or physiotherapists would
need to continue a line of responsibility outside
the team, and to meet with their professional colleagues outside the team for their own support and
development. In large teams, the teacher-in-charge
may need a deputy and team teachers may need to be
on two scales. It may also be a good idea to retain
a small proportion of posts for one year secondments
for teachers from local schools. This would provide
an in-service function, as well as giving the team
a basis in a local school once the seconded teacher
had returned, for helping the school to bring about
its own organisational changes.
     In a large team it may also be necessary to
give special responsibility to one post for in-
service training. This would involve planning the
in-service for members of the team and the team's
own in-service initiatives with schools. To prevent
undue specialisation developing within the team,
it might be best for the in-service responsibility
to rotate between senior team members on an annual
or biennial basis.
     Another aspect of the service would be the in-
clusion and co-ordination of specialist support
teachers (particularly of the sensory handicapped)
into a team of largely generic support teachers. These
specialist teachers would have a teaching and support
role to some of the designated special classes in
ordinary schools, especially where they were part-
time, as well as to individual pupils and their

teachers in ordinary classes. Indeed, the specialist teachers may be called in by the team to help with assessments and, thereby, take a part in shaping the referral to them of pupils for specialist teaching. This would reduce the emotional isolation of many specialist teachers, without taking them away from professional accountability to specialist advisers.

The responsibility of allocation of teachers' time to schools would lie with the teacher-in-charge. Thus, he or she would devote as much time to external relations as to internal relations. If there were no reorganisation of existing special needs teaching in schools, the question of ensuring that that teaching was given, and how, would remain. As previously argued above, heads of schools may find it difficult to give it priority. Assuming that some of the pupils involved may be the subject of full assessment statements, a more direct responsibility would devolve on the authority to supervise the teaching. If the Special Education Adviser did not have the time, this responsibility may be passed onto or shared with the teacher-in-charge of the support service.

Where an area needed a large team (more than 20), it may be best to split the team into two or three. Such a split could follow three variations. One would be on a geographical basis. This would have the difficulty that it might encourage rivalry between the sub-teams, and put the teacher-in-charge in a difficult position to keep control, especially if such sub-teams were in different bases. As far as possible the geographical entity of the team should match that of the administration of the authority. Another variation would be to split the team according to specialisms - learning, behaviour, curriculum development, etc. However, this would lose sight of one of the main theoretical tenets of a Support Service - that special needs are to do with whole children, in integrated classes, in whole schools. The interaction between factors (individual, peer group, teachers, parents, school) is at the very heart of the challenge and stimulus that face teachers in ordinary schools.

The third variation on subdividing a team would be on an age-range basis. If two teams were required a primary-secondary split seems logical, with the proviso that teachers who know pupils in the last year of junior school would be able, if necessary, to follow them to the end of their first year of secondary school. If three teams were required, an infant-junior-secondary split may work, again with the proviso of teachers being able to follow pupils

till the end of the first year in the next stage.
These arrangements would mirror the many other systems
in an authority which split along these lines whilst
ensuring successful communication between levels. It
may also facilitate the attachment of specialist teachers or professionals to the team. For example,
speech therapists might have most to do with the
infant sub-team, and specific learning difficulties
teachers with the junior sub-team.

If special needs teaching is going to develop,
whether school-based or team-based, the role of educational psychologists is likely to change. It has
already changed with the implementation of the 1981
Act, in that more time is now needed for the assessment and administration of the paperwork for each
child who may need special education. Special needs
teachers are likely to get involved in the assessment of pupils and would be in a good position, from
the point of view of time, to carry out criterion-
referenced assessments. There will clearly still be
a need for specialised educational assessments which
only trained educational psychologists will be able
to perform, and for psychological assessments.

If the assessment load of psychologists is
lightened (fewer referrals), this should free time
for other activities, which most psychologists now
perform in differing proportions. Amongst these are
individual and group consultation for teachers. This
would be one aspect of the work of an educational
psychologist attached to a Support Service. Another
is systems work, which involves working with whole
systems in schools, which would be affected by a
policy of integration. Finally, psychologists have
been trained in the evaluation of educational performance, and this is a function that is vital to
the growth and development of a Support Service.

The management committee of the team would need
to reflect its composition and responsibilities
whilst remaining as small as possible. The person in
the best position to chair the committee would be the
Special Education Adviser. Also represented on the
committee might be the Education Officer, the Educational Psychologists, and any other professional group,
and the teaching body of the team, in the persons of
the teacher-in-charge and a teacher representative.
The management committee would also draw on the
opinion and advice of representative primary and
secondary heads, and community representatives. It
would be helpful also to have some parental representation on the management committee.

The role and function of support services

This chapter took as its starting-off point the integration of children with special educational needs in ordinary school. It has sought to look at the administrative implications of such a policy. In so doing, it is clear that the policy would affect every system, both educational and administrative, within an LEA. The chapter has considered the role of specialist teachers, the practice of support teaching, the notion of a new kind of support teacher - a generic learning support teacher, the organisation and control of support services, the various needs for in-service training, and the importance of evaluation. The final chapter will examine how changes can be brought about to improve support for children with special needs and their teachers in mainstream schools.

Chapter 7

THE CHALLENGE OF DISRUPTIVE BEHAVIOUR

It is very easy, when referring to classroom disruption, to make it seem uniform, all of one kind. It is even easier, when referring to a pupil whose behaviour is disruptive, to think of him or her as disruptive. The ascription of the label 'disruptive' can be made as generally as common adjectives like naughty, bright, or lazy, or it can be made into a pseudo-psychological word like maladjusted or disturbed. The usage has become loose, and the hidden assumptions behind the word can shift imperceptibly. A 'disruptive pupil' comes to mean a pupil who can indulge in any sort of behaviour that a teacher finds problematical for the purposes of teaching and, moreover, is liable to do so at any time, in any circumstances. For this reason, such pupils have special teachers to deal with them, who have special methods, so the train of inference goes.

Throughout this book, care has been taken to refer to disruptive behaviour and not to disruptive pupils, to stress and illustrate the importance of context and of situation to give meaning to the disruptive behaviour. It is still easy to think of some behaviour eg. shouting out in class as similar from school to school. Of course, there are similarities, but their causes and their interventions will be likely to reveal wide differences. Equally, it is easy to think that, if a pupil shows one type of disruptive behaviour, such as refusing to work in one situation, he or she is somehow likely to show another type of disruptive behaviour, such as picking a fight. Clearly, there are correlations between different types of disruptive behaviour, and these may be linked to individual psychological or social factors. The view taken here is that, whatever the individual psychology of the child, then disruptive behaviour is a challenge which states

173

that learning is not taking place in that given situation, and that it is in the power of teachers and administrators to change that situation to try and help the learning process. The challenge of disruptive behaviour does not call for large scale dramatic gestures by authorities. Data are not available to show whether the intensity of disruptive behaviour at present in schools is a new phenomenon or not. Historical evidence from public and elementary schools in the nineteenth century suggests that it is not new. What is new is the publicity that it has received politically and in the media, and the responses that authorities have made to it. The challenge of disruptive behaviour is to change. But change which is purely reactive can simply become part of the problem. Change needs planning. Planning is a process that needs a method. If there is a prescriptive message in this book, it is not necessarily to copy the procedures and techniques that we have described and evaluated in Chapters 2 to 5. It is to agree on a method of analysis, and to stick to it. We shall conclude by summarising this method, and by considering its applicability at four different levels - the pupil, the classroom, the school, and the LEA.

7.1 Levels of change.

The prevention of disruption will come from change at different levels, perhaps simultaneously, perhaps sequentially. Change at one level is likely to be visible to practitioners at the same level and at a level connected to it. If changes lead to successful results, then they are likely to be copied. It is possible to think of change being initiated from the top of a hierarchy, or developing from below. An example of each of these may serve to show how resistance must be foreseen and worked through at other levels. When a local education authority makes a decision to transform the staff of three disruptive units into a peripatetic team to work in its twenty secondary schools, that is a top directed change. The new team will, inevitably, meet resistance from head teachers and classroom teachers who may see a threat to their existing policies and practices. When a classteacher determines to develop strategies to manage classroom disruption in his or her own lessons, and not to refer children any longer to the head of year, this is change developing from below. The change will mean a shift in the roles and responsibilities of the head of year, or at least he

or she will have time to direct energies elsewhere.
At the same time, the classroom teacher may be calling for other types of resource, like more ancillary
help, or parental involvement, or advice from specialist teachers. These demands will eventually press
for change in the school as a whole, and in the
education authority's allocation of resources.

7.2 A model for change.

It is important to stress that what is being
advocated in this book is not simply the establishment of peripatetic teams to work with the issue of
classroom disruption. What is being suggested is a
model of working that has five main components:
referral, assessment, formulation, intervention, and
evaluation. This model can be applied at different
levels - the pupil, the classroom, the school, and
the LEA. It's strength is that it can take account of
how change at one level affects others. The following synopsis draws attention to the main considerations at each stage.

7.2.1 The referral stage.

1. The first question is to clarify what the
   difficulty is. The whole process of change
   is a continual debate around this first
   question.

2. This clarification may need to be extended
   to persons beyond those who refer the difficulty. At an early stage, this may simply
   be keeping people at different levels informed. Later, intervention may involve them
   in changes. For example in the referral of
   disruptive behaviour the discussion of the
   problem will need to be extended beyond the
   referring teacher to the head teacher, other
   teachers, or to parents or pupils.

3. The process itself of clarification is one
   of sometimes loosening and sometimes tightening concepts, questioning assumptions,
   but not questioning observations.

4. This questioning is the start of attitudinal
   change, but it is not enough by itself. In
   fact, behavioural change brought about by
   intervention often precedes attitudinal
   change. However, attitudes must change, if

behavioural changes are to be maintained.

5. It is not necessary to pinpoint the 'real' difficulty straight away. One aim is to help in sharing the perceived difficulty and easing communication between different people involved in it. This will often mean communication across levels. For instance, at LEA level, there may be a problem of the co-ordination of in-service training. The referral stage may concentrate on helping people to communicate who do not normally do so, such as the teachers who never attend any in-service, and the advisers who organise it.

7.2.2 The assessment stage.

1. Clarify that there is going to be an agreed assessment process upon which intervention will be based. Estimate a time period for it.

2. Elicit ideas about the methods of the assessment with the participants. Keep people at different levels informed. If working with a school or LEA, consult with the person in charge first and, thereafter, keep people informed both vertically and horizontally in a hierarchy.
   The assessment will usually involve some of the following: discussion, interview, observation, questionnaire, and so be familiar with and plan in-service training in these techniques.
   The more people involved, the more the work of assessment can be shared, provided that tasks are agreed and scheduled beforehand.

3. Try to be systematic and objective. This can only be built up over time as procedures evolve and as a common vocabulary is reached. The objectivity of the language of behavioural analysis has proved helpful in this respect.

4. Try to achieve an agreement on method first rather than on early conclusions that are being drawn.

7.2.3 <u>The formulation stage.</u>

1. By this stage, it should be clear with whom
   one is working, be it one pupil, a group of
   pupils, one teacher, a group of teachers,
   or a working party within the LEA. Everyone
   in their heads will have some formulation
   of the difficulty, but not everyone will be
   able to put down on paper precisely what the
   problem is, and why and how it occurs.

2. The process of formulation is that of putting forward a hypothesis to be tested by
   experience. At worst, one should write it down
   for oneself. At best, one should arrive at
   it jointly with the person(s) with whom one
   is working.

3. A formulation can be revised at any stage
   in the light of experience.

7.2.4 <u>The intervention stage.</u>

1. The intervention should follow logically
   from the formulation. Where a range of interventions are possible, choose at LEA level
   the one involving the smallest commitment
   of time and least disturbance of routine.

2. The objectives of intervention need to be
   stated at the outset. It may not be possible
   to achieve all the objectives at once. Only
   proceed with those that are agreed by all,
   and those which are practicable.

3. Agree on the length of intervention.

4. Specify a means of evaluating the intervention and a date for reviewing it.

5. Agree on tasks in carrying out intervention
   and offer regular support throughout.

6. Expect institutional resistance to change,
   especially if intervention starts successfully. Acknowledge the resistance, but continue encouraging the motivation to change
   rather than becoming resentful of lack of
   commitment. Try to minimise resistance by
   consulting different levels about the intervention and by keeping them informed of

progress.

7.2.5 Evaluation stage.

1. This is the corner-stone of the whole process. If evaluation is built in from the
   start, then all of the preceding stages must
   be included.

2. The most important aspect is commitment to
   the methods of evaluation. The method will
   be likely to be similar to or, in some
   cases, a direct replication of the assessment process.
   If observation or questionnaire data have
   been collected, they can be repeated. The
   comparison of data creates a framework for
   objectivity.

3. For large-scale interventions - with whole
   schools, or with organisational systems -
   it may be best to appoint an evaluator who
   is outside the school or system. The role
   of such a person is not to adjudicate success
   or failure, but to try to understand what
   has taken place, and to feed that back to
   the participants for them to draw their
   own conclusions.

4. For small-scale interventions, such as minor
   changes in a teacher's handling of a child,
   it is easy to overlook evaluation, or to
   pass it over with comments like 'things seem
   a bit better now'. It is important to carry
   out evaluation formally in the way and at
   the time that was agreed beforehand. Successful intervention is just as difficult to
   absorb as unsuccessful, because both mean
   change.

5. The results of evaluation should be fed back
   to all participants, and should be accessible for scrutiny. The process of feedback
   is eased, if everyone has agreed in the
   first place on methods of assessment and
   evaluation.

7.3 Resources for change.

The ideas and working methods outlined in Chapters 4, 5, and 6 could be translated into policy proposals at classroom, school, and LEA levels. The objection usually made to any new policy proposal is that it is impossible to implement because it will cost too much. This may be just another example of resistance to change.

It needs to be emphasised that what is being recommended as good practice likely to prevent classroom disruption is not necessarily a set of policies which will involve increased expenditure. In the first place, many of the changes suggested in classroom practice (in Chapter 4) and schools (in Chapter 5) could be carried out by teachers already working in schools with a minimum of support. As we have stressed, much of what we are recommending is little more than good practice as it already exists in some schools. Further, to the extent that we are advocating additional support staff in schools or in peripatetic support teams, this may not involve additional funding. The resources for support are already being spent in many LEA's. Unfortunately, they are being spent in order to prolong the life of segregated special provision via the proliferation of disruptive units and the myriad forms of special classes (Lloyd-Smith, M. [Ed.], 1984). As indicated in Chapter 1 this policy has the effect of stigmatising huge numbers of children, and condemning them to an inferior education. Furthermore, it is unsuccessful in preventing classroom disruption. The more children are removed from a school, the more the school wants to be removed. This policy needs not merely to be stopped, but to be reversed. Resources need to be shifted from special schools units and classes back into the mainstream classroom.

Finding the funds for support teachers, then, is largely a matter of using existing resources flexibly. The money spent on off-site units could be better used to purchase support teachers who could work with mainstream teachers in schools. In many cases the personnel who currently work in segregated provision might be the ones with the necessary expertise to work as support teachers. The fact that some of these teachers have actually transformed their method of working from being guardians of sin bins into being in-school support teachers indicates that many would be only too pleased to see such changes in their role. In the case of on-site units such changes can be made reasonably easily.

7.4 Changing education.

Some of the suggestions in this book might come under the slightly disdainful heading of tips for teachers. The suggestion for classroom management in Chapter 4, for instance, might fall into this category. However, most of the suggestions address more fundamentally many of the practices of schools and teachers. Changing schools to prevent classroom disruption is actually to change the nature of the education system. This is even more apparent if the integration of pupils perceived to be disruptive is considered alongside those others perceived to have special educational needs (see Chapters 1 and 6). To integrate these pupils would need fundamental changes in classrooms and schools which would influence the education of all children. Both the integration and the accompanying necessary changes would benefit the education of all children. This process is already beginning and can be developed at different levels, as indicated earlier in the chapter. It represents one of the positive directions in education in the UK at present.

Integrating children with special needs is not a 'cure' for their needs. In a way, it is the techniques of intervention which we have illustrated which benefit the pupils referred. It is the education they continue to receive in mainstream schools which is their real benefit. A successful and positive experience of education alongside peers is the ultimate antidote to classroom disruption. The aim of support teaching is not to try to usurp the education of referred pupils, but rather to help them to benefit as soon as possible from the education offered in schools. This can only be achieved if education changes to be more responsive to the individual needs of all children.

REFERENCES

(For comprehensive bibliographies and literature reviews see Skinner, A. et al., 1983, and Topping, K.J., 1983.)

Bash, L., Coulby, D., Jones, C. (1985) Urban Schooling: Theory & Practice, Cassells, London.

Berger, M. (1979) 'Behaviour modification in education and professional practice: the dangers of mindless technology', Bulletin Brit. Psychol. Soc., 32, 418-419.

Berger, M. & Wigley, V. (1980) 'Intervening in the Classroom', ILEA Contact, 9, 13, p.4.

Booth, T. (1982) Special Biographies, Open University Press, Milton Keynes.

Booth, T. & Potts, P. (eds.) (1983) Integrating Special Education, Blackwell, Oxford.

Bowman, I. (1981) 'Maladjustment: a history of the category', in Swann, W. (ed.), 1981, op. cit.

Central Advisory Council for Education (England) (1967) Children and Their Primary Schools: A Report, (2 Vols.), The Plowden Report, HMSO, London.

Corrigan, P. (1979) Schooling the Smash Street Kids, Macmillan, London.

Coulby, D. (1984) 'Intervening in Classrooms', invited paper delivered at ACPP annual conference.

Coulby, D. (1984) 'The Creation of the Disruptive Pupil', in Lloyd Smith, M. (ed.) 1984 op. cit.

Coulby D. & Harper, T. (1982) 'Support in the Disrupted Classroom', JABAC, 5, 2, 22-27.

Davie, R. et al. (1972) From Birth to Seven, Longman, London.

D.E.S. (1978) Special Educational Needs: Report of the Committee of Enquiry into the Education of Handicapped Children and Young People, (The Warnock Report) HMSO, London.

Department of Education and Science (1981) West Indian Children in Our Schools: Interim Report of the Committee of Enquiry into the Education of Children from Ethnic Minority Groups, Cmnd. 8273 (The Rampton Report), HMSO, London.

Evans, B. & Waites, B. (1981) IQ and Mental Testing, Macmillan, London.

References

Ghodsias, M. (1977) 'Children's Behaviour and the BSAG', British Journal of Social & Clinical Psychology, 16, 1, 23-28.

Gipps, C. & Gross, H. (1983)'LEA policies in Identification and Provision for Children with Special Educational Needs in Ordinary Schools', University of London Institute of Education unpublished paper.

Halsey, A.H. et al (1980) Origins and Destinations, Oxford University Press, Oxford.

Hammersley, M. & Woods, P. (eds.) (1976) The Process of Schooling, Open University Press, Milton Keynes.

Hargreaves, D.H. (1982) The Challenge for the Comprehensive School: culture, curriculum and community, Routledge & Kegan Paul, London.

Hargreaves, D.H. et al. (1984) Improving Secondary Schools, ILEA, London.

Harper, T. (1984) 'The effects of transfer to secondary school on disruptive behaviour', unpublished paper.

Harrop, A. (1983) Behaviour Modification in the Classroom, Hodder & Stoughton, London.

Hegarty, S. & Pocklington, K. (1981) Educating Pupils With Special Needs in the Ordinary School, NFER-Nelson, Windsor.

Hegarty, S. & Pocklington, K. (1982) Integration in Action: Case Studies in the Integration of Pupils with Special Needs, NFER-Nelson, Windsor.

H.M.I. (1978) Behavioural Units, HMSO, London.

Homme, L. et al. (1970) How to Use Contingency Contracting in the Classroom, Research Press, New York.

Kamin, L.J. (1974) The Science and Politics of IQ, John Wiley, New York.

Lane, D. (1978a; 1978b) The Impossible Child, Volumes 1 & 2, ILEA, London.

Leach, D.J. & Raybould, E.C. (1979) Learning and Behaviour Difficulties in School, Open Books, London.

Lloyd Smith, M. (ed.) (1984) Disruptive Schooling, John Murray, London.

McManus, M. (1982) 'Raise Eyebrows not Fists', TES, 10.9.82, No. 3454.

Mortimore, P. et al. (1983) Behaviour Problems in Schools: An Evaluation of Support Centres, Croom Helm, London.

Rediguides, School of Education, University of Nottingham.

References

Rosser, E. & Harre, R. (1976) 'The meaning of "trouble" ', in Hammersley, M. and Woods, P. (1976) The Process of Schooling, Routledge & Kegan Paul, London.

Rutter M. et al. (1979) Fifteen Thousand Hours, Open Books, London.

Skinner, A. et al. (1983) Disaffection from School: Issues and Interagency Responses, National Youth Bureau, Leicester.

Stott, D.H. (1974) The Bristol Social Adjustment Guide: Manual, Hodder & Stoughton, London.

Stott, D.H. (1983) Issues in the Intelligence Debate, NFER-Nelson, Windsor.

Swann, W. (ed.) (1981) The Practice of Special Education, Blackwell, London.

Tomlinson, S. (1981) Educational Subnormality - A Study in Decision Making, Routledge & Kegan Paul, London.

Topping, K.J. (1983) Educational Systems for Disruptive Adolescents, Croom Helm, London.

Wheldall, K. (ed.) (1981)'The Behaviourist in the Classroom: Aspects of Applied Behavioural Analysis in British Educational Contexts', University of Birmingham Faculty of Education, Birmingham.

Whitty, G. (1981) 'Special Units: a force for change or control', J. for Workers in Social Ed. Centres, No. 1, 14-22.

Yule, W. (1968) 'The Child and the Outside World', Paper given to the annual conference of the Association of Special Education.

APPENDIX

Some indications from statistical analysis of factors
which may influence outcome of intervention.

        With the variables available, it was possible
to consider whether any of them correlated significantly with any of the outcome measures. The main
variables that were considered for this were sex,
age at referral, severity of referral, length of intervention, and type of intervention. Because the
nature of the experimental design was a multiple
single case design, it was important to realise that
any comparison between groups derived from these
variables would only be open to correlation analysis.
Lacking control groups, it would not be possible to
draw any conclusions about causation. Nevertheless,
some variables were found to correlate significantly
with some outcomes.

Sex.
        It will be remembered that 76% of the referrals
were boys. It was found that there was no significant difference on outcome scores between boys and
girls. However, when age was taken into account,
differences were found. A higher proportion of girls
were referred at secondary age and, in fact, at the
ages of 14 and 15 the ratio was almost 1:2, compared
to 1:3 overall. The outcome scores showed that the
behaviour of girls of infant age changed more on
BSAG scores than of boys of infant age. Also, at
secondary age, the BSAG scores showed that the behaviour of girls was seen to change less than that of
boys. These differences did not reach a significant
level on the other outcome measures (Checklist differences and behaviour change ratings).

Appendix

Age.
These differences between boys and girls might
be thought to reflect simply the different ratios
of referral of boys and girls at different ages.
However, the only outcome score on which age did
prove significant (p<0.05) was on the rating of behaviour change, on which infant pupils of either
sex were rated as having changed significantly more
than juniors or secondary pupils. Clearly, the three
outcome measures may be more or less sensitive to
different aspects of a teacher's perception of pupil
behaviour. The sex and age differences are important
to monitor because of the implications for allocation
of support teacher time.

Severity of referral.
The cases were categorised for severity according to the Ovract score on the first BSAG. The range
of scores for the referral population was divided
into quartiles to give four categories of severity,
a fifth category was also created of all cases which
scored in the most severe category (4) on Ovract and
within the first quartile of the range of scores on
Unract. These five categories were then analysed
according to outcome scores, also taking into account
the type of school. It was found that, for all three
types of school, the more severe the case as measured by the initial Ovract score, the greater the
change in behaviour as measured by the outcome scores
on the BSAG differences and the Checklist differences. In other words, a pupil whose initial BSAG
Ovract score was high would be perceived to change
more than a pupil whos initial score was low. There
are two probable explanations for this. Firstly,
a high score gives more scope for change than a low
score. Secondly, it may be the case that all teachers have a tolerance threshold for disruptive behaviour that is related to their ability to cope as
much as the actual behaviour of the pupil. If a
pupil's behaviour goes even a little beyond this
threshold, he or she is likely to be referred. The
act of referral may make the teacher perceive the
pupil's behaviour to be more severe than it actually
is. The intervention may have two effects. Firstly,
for the less severe cases, it may not actually need
much behaviour change for it to fall back below the
teacher's threshold. This may account for the less
severe case being perceived to have changed less.
Secondly, for the more severe cases, the behaviour
may change considerably, but also the teacher's
threshold may be raised. Since the act of closing

a case is usually an implicit statement by the teachers in school that they can cope, this may be justified by their thinking that if this were a severe case, and that they can now cope, then he or she must have changed a great deal.

Finally, there was one more interesting finding related to severity. Those cases with high Ovract score and high Unract score on initial BSAG were perceived on all outcome measures to change disruptive behaviour less than those cases simply with high Ovract scores. In other words, a child who at times acts out and at times is rather withdrawn and unforthcoming may be more resistant to change than a child who simply spends most of the time acting out. At least, a high Unract score is a signal of difficulty and a signal that factors outside the immediate classroom situation may be relevant in explaining why the pupil's behaviour is different at different times in the same classroom situation.

Length of intervention.

The length of intervention in terms of the number of weeks of school time between the referral and the closure of a case was analysed according to the three measures of outcome. It was found that the length of intervention did not make a difference to outcome, i.e. interventions of only six weeks' duration were no more or less successful than interventions of thirty-six weeks. It is clear that some decision process was going on that meant that interventions were contined as long as was necessary to bring about a conclusion that either satisfactory progress had been made, or that no further progress could be made.

Type of intervention.

The final variable that was investigated because it may have a bearing on outcome was the nature of the intervention. It will be clear from Chapters 2 and 4 that the type of intervention was quite varied, and often consisted of combinations of work with an individual pupil, with a group of pupils, with a teacher, and with parents. By looking at the frequencies of different combinations of intervention, it was found that the combinations could be placed into the following categories: work with the teacher only, work with the teacher and the child, work with the teacher, child and parents, work with the teacher, child and peer group. It could be hypothesised that a certain type of work would be more successful than others. In fact, the analysis of outcomes according to these categories of intervention found no significant differences. This points to the possibility that interventions, since they are all on average equally successful, are carefully matched to the needs of the case, by the process of assessment and formulation.